A Record of Discovery for
Exploring
Computers

Fourth Edition

Gary B. Shelly
Thomas J. Cashman
Tim J. Walker

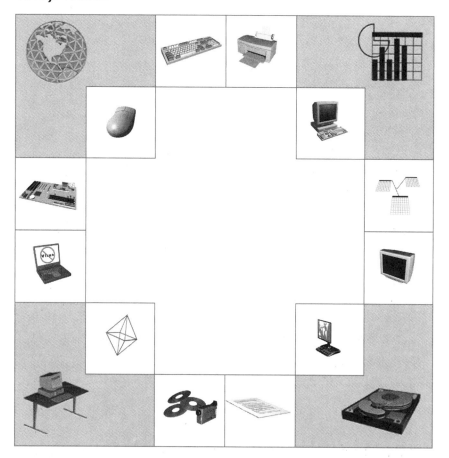

COURSE TECHNOLOGY
THOMSON LEARNING

COURSE TECHNOLOGY
25 THOMSON PLACE
BOSTON MA 02210

SHELLY CASHMAN SERIES.

Australia • Canada • Denmark • Japan • Mexico • New Zealand • Philippines • Puerto Rico • Singapore
South Africa • Spain • United Kingdom • United States

COURSE TECHNOLOGY
★
™
THOMSON LEARNING

Asia (excluding Japan)
Thomson Learning
60 Albert Street, #15-01
Albert Complex
Singapore 189969

Japan
Thomson Learning
Palaceside Building 5F
1-1-1 Hitotsubashi, Chiyoda-ku
Tokyo 100 0003 Japan

Australia/New Zealand
Nelson/Thomson Learning
102 Dodds Street
South Melbourne, Victoria 3205
Australia

Latin America
Thomson Learning
Seneca, 53
Colonia Polanco
11560 Mexico D.F. Mexico

South Africa
Thomson Learning
Zonnebloem Building,
Constantia Square
526 Sixteenth Road
P.O. Box 2459
Halfway House, 1685
South Africa

Canada
Nelson/Thomson Learning
1120 Birchmount Road
Scarborough, Ontario
Canada M1K 5G4

UK/Europe/Middle East
Thomson Learning
Berkshire House
168-173 High Holborn
London, WC1V 7AA United Kingdom

Spain
Thomson Learning
Calle Magallanes, 25
28015-MADRID
ESPANA

DISCLAIMER

ISBN 0-7895-6372-X (Textbook)
ISBN 0-7895-6373-8 (Textbook and CD-ROM)
ISBN 0-7895-6111-5 (CD-ROM)

1 2 3 4 5 6 7 8 9 10   BC   06 05 04 03 02

Contents

Contents

Contents

Preface

A Record of Discovery for Exploring Computers, Fourth Edition is a journal in which students chronicle, analyze, and extend their experiences with computer concepts. The journal may be used with either the *Exploring Computers* CD-ROM or the Shelly Cashman Series Interactive Labs on CD-ROM. Students investigate an interactive lab once on their own and then use this journal as they study the lab a second time. A variety of activities are provided in a format that is easy to follow and facilitates learning, helping students independently master introductory computer concepts. Each lab section in *A Record of Discovery for Exploring Computers, Fourth Edition* consists of four major parts:

- **Summarizing the Lab** reviews content, shows relationships, and provides additional facts in an outline that students complete as they work through the lab.
- **Evaluating the Results** tests students on their mastery of the material presented in the lab using four types of objective questions: True/False, Matching, Multiple Choice, and Fill in the Blank.
- **Examining the Issues** challenges students to consider some interesting questions related to the lab and express their views on these intriguing problems.
- **Investigating the World** gives students the opportunity to leave the classroom and learn how people use, market, and are affected by computers.

Interspersed throughout Summarizing the Lab are features especially designed to further students' comprehension of the material presented. *Exploring Windows* scrutinizes each topic using the Microsoft Windows operating system. *Exploring Online* suggests ways the Internet can be used to gain more information. *Exploring Your Computer* encourages students to find out more about the PC they are using.

All these elements combined provide a unique learning experience.

Acknowledgments

The Shelly Cashman Series would not be the leading computer education series without the contributions of outstanding publishing professionals. First, and foremost, among them is Becky Herrington, director of production and designer. She is the heart and soul of the Shelly Cashman Series, and it is only through her leadership, dedication, and tireless efforts that superior products are made possible. Becky created and produced the award-winning Windows series of books.

Under Becky's direction, the following individuals made significant contributions to these books: Doug Cowley, production manager; Ginny Harvey, series specialist and developmental editor; Ken Russo, senior Web and graphic designer; Mike Bodnar, associate production manager; Mark Norton, Web designer; Meena Moest, product review manager, Bruce Greene, multimedia product manager; Michelle Linder, Christy Otten, Chris Schneider, and Ryan Ung, graphic artists; Jeanne Black and Betty Hopkins, Quark experts; Lyn Markowicz, Nancy Lamm, Kim Kosmatka, and Eva Kandarpa, copyeditors/proofreaders; Cristina Haley, proofreader/indexer; and Richard Herrera, cover design.

Finally, we would like to thank Richard Keaveny, associate publisher; John Sisson, managing editor; Jim Quasney, series consulting editor; Erin Runyon, associate product manager; Francis Schurgot and Marc Ouellette, Web product managers; Rachel VanKirk, marketing manager; and Reed Cotter, editorial assistant.

Gary B. Shelly
Thomas J. Cashman
Tim J. Walker

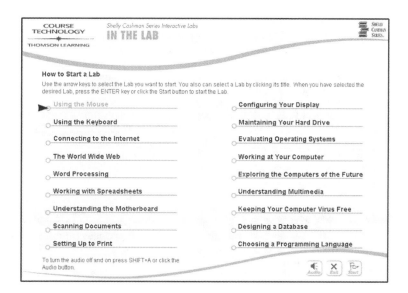

Shelly Cashman Series – Traditionally Bound Textbooks

The Shelly Cashman Series presents the following computer subjects in a variety of traditionally bound textbooks. For more information, see your Course Technology representative or call 1-800-648-7450. For Shelly Cashman Series information, visit Shelly Cashman Online at **scseries.com**

COMPUTERS	
Computers	Discovering Computers 2002: Concepts for a Digital World, Web Enhanced, Complete Edition
	Discovering Computers 2002: Concepts for a Digital World, Web Enhanced, Introductory Edition
	Discovering Computers 2002: Concepts for a Digital World, Web Enhanced, Brief Edition
	Teachers Discovering Computers: Integrating Technology in the Classroom 2e
	Exploring Computers: A Record of Discovery 4e
	Study Guide for Discovering Computers 2002: Concepts for a Digital World, Web Enhanced
	Essential Introduction to Computers 4e (32-page)

WINDOWS APPLICATIONS	
Microsoft Office	Microsoft Office XP: Essential Concepts and Techniques (5 projects)
	Microsoft Office XP: Brief Concepts and Techniques (9 projects)
	Microsoft Office XP: Introductory Concepts and Techniques (15 projects)
	Microsoft Office XP: Advanced Concepts and Techniques (11 projects)
	Microsoft Office XP: Post Advanced Concepts and Techniques (11 projects)
	Microsoft Office 2000: Essential Concepts and Techniques (5 projects)
	Microsoft Office 2000: Brief Concepts and Techniques (9 projects)
	Microsoft Office 2000: Introductory Concepts and Techniques, Enhanced Edition (15 projects)
	Microsoft Office 2000: Advanced Concepts and Techniques (11 projects)
	Microsoft Office 2000: Post Advanced Concepts and Techniques (11 projects)
Integration	Integrating Microsoft Office XP Applications and the World Wide Web: Essential Concepts and Techniques
PIM	Microsoft Outlook 2002: Essential Concepts and Techniques
Microsoft Works	Microsoft Works 6: Complete Concepts and Techniques[1] • Microsoft Works 2000: Complete Concepts and Techniques[1] • Microsoft Works 4.5[1]
Microsoft Windows	Microsoft Windows 2000: Complete Concepts and Techniques (6 projects)[2]
	Microsoft Windows 2000: Brief Concepts and Techniques (2 projects)
	Microsoft Windows 98: Essential Concepts and Techniques (2 projects)
	Microsoft Windows 98: Complete Concepts and Techniques (6 projects)[2]
	Introduction to Microsoft Windows NT Workstation 4
	Microsoft Windows 95: Complete Concepts and Techniques[1]
Word Processing	Microsoft Word 2002[2] • Microsoft Word 2000[2] • Microsoft Word 97[1] • Microsoft Word 7[1]
Spreadsheets	Microsoft Excel 2002[2] • Microsoft Excel 2000[2] • Microsoft Excel 97[1] • Microsoft Excel 7[1] • Microsoft Excel 5[1]
Database	Microsoft Access 2002[2] • Microsoft Access 2000[2] • Microsoft Access 97[1] • Microsoft Access 7[1]
Presentation Graphics	Microsoft PowerPoint 2002[2] • Microsoft PowerPoint 2000[2] • Microsoft PowerPoint 97[1] • Microsoft PowerPoint 7[1]
Desktop Publishing	Microsoft Publisher 2002[1] • Microsoft Publisher 2000[1]

PROGRAMMING	
Programming	Microsoft Visual Basic 6: Complete Concepts and Techniques[1] • Programming in QBasic
	Java Programming: Complete Concepts and Techniques[1] • Structured COBOL Programming 2e

INTERNET	
Browser	Microsoft Internet Explorer 5: An Introduction • Microsoft Internet Explorer 4: An Introduction
	Netscape Navigator 6: An Introduction • Netscape Navigator 4: An Introduction
Web Page Creation and Design	Web Design: Introductory Concepts and Techniques • HTML: Complete Concepts and Techniques[1]
	Microsoft FrontPage 2002: Essential Concepts and Techniques • Microsoft FrontPage 2002[2]
	Microsoft FrontPage 2000[1] • JavaScript: Complete Concepts and Techniques[1]

SYSTEMS ANALYSIS	
Systems Analysis	Systems Analysis and Design 4e

DATA COMMUNICATIONS	
Data Communications	Business Data Communications: Introductory Concepts and Techniques 3e

[1]Also available as an Introductory Edition, which is a shortened version of the complete book
[2]Also available as an Introductory Edition, which is a shortened version of the complete book and also as a Comprehensive Edition, which is an extended version of the complete book

A RECORD OF DISCOVERY for Exploring Computers

FOURTH EDITION

1-1

Using the Mouse

Summarizing the Lab

1

Instructions: Use the *Using the Mouse* interactive lab to complete the following outline.

I. What is a mouse?

A mouse is a unique _____ that fits in the palm of the hand.

Because it is used to enter data into a computer, a mouse is an example of an input device. Keyboards and scanners also are input devices.

In a graphical user interface (GUI) like Microsoft Windows , a mouse is used to select options and to move items on the screen.

II. The mouse and Windows

Windows uses features such as icons, windows, menus, and buttons.

- An _____ is a small graphical symbol that represents a computer program, application or document.

- A_____ is a rectangular area that presents information about an application, program, or document;

- A _____ is a list of related options about an application, program, or document.

Exploring Online

Early Internet software could be controlled only by using the keyboard. With modern Internet software, including web browsers such as Microsoft Internet Explorer and Netscape Navigator, people can access text, graphics, and other types of media by pointing and clicking the mouse. The Yahoo! home page includes a listing of home pages devoted to mouse devices and mouse accessories such as mouse pads and mouse boards. Companies such as Logitech also include pictures of different types of mouse devices on their Web sites. To learn more about using a mouse, visit the Exploring Computers Web page (www.scsite.com/expl.htm) and click Mouse.

- A _____ is a rectangular, circular, or other type of icon that causes an action to take place when clicked.

III. Mouse operations

The primary advantage of a mouse is that it is easy to use.

The Mouse is used to perform four basic operations: pointing, clicking, double-clicking, and dragging.

A. _____ is moving the mouse across the mouse pad or desk surface to control the movement of a mouse pointer (often a block arrow).

An electromechanical mouse has a small ball in its base. When the ball moves, a signal is sent to the computer and the mouse pointer moves accordingly. An optical mouse contains a minicamera. As the mouse moves across the surface of a special grid, the position of the mouse is conveyed to the computer.

Trackballs and joysticks also can control the movement of the mouse pointer.

> ### Exploring Your Computer
> Examine the mouse you are using to work through these labs. Do you have an optical mouse or electromechanical mouse? Does it have one, two, or three buttons? Does it have a wheel button? Are you using a mouse pad to protect your mouse from dirt and dust?

B. _____ is pressing and releasing a button on the mouse.

A mouse has two or more buttons that can be pressed. A mouse also can have a combination _____ , which can be rotated like a wheel or clicked like a standard mouse button.

A typical mouse has a left button and a right button.

- The _____ functions to select objects, graphics, or icons, as well as to move objects
Pressing the left button is referred to as _____.

- The _____ functions to open shortcut menus that are specific to an object, screen region, or application.
Pressing the right button is referred to as _____.

C. _____ is pointing to an object and quickly pressing and releasing the left mouse button twice. This is used to open a file or start an application.

Software applications such as Windows allow users to adjust the double-click speed of the mouse.

Exploring Windows

In Windows, users can right-click files, programs, and other objects to display shortcut menus (menus that apply to a specific window or situation). These menus may include commands for cutting, copying, pasting, opening, or performing a variety of other functions on each object.

D. _____ combines the operations of pointing to an item, holding down the left mouse button, moving the mouse, and then releasing the button in order to move the item on the screen.

_____ is like dragging, but you hold down the right mouse button and a shortcut menu displays when the button is released.

IV. Manipulating user interface controls

The mouse can be used to select options and choose commands. In Windows, you use the Mouse Properties dialog box to adjust or customize mouse features. To display the Mouse Properties dialog box:

1. Click the _____ on the bottom left corner of the screen. The Start menu displays. The Start menu is the most basic menu in Windows

2. Point to the Settings command and then choose the _____ on the submenu to open the Control Panel window.

3. Double-click the _____ in the Control Panel window to display the Mouse Properties dialog box.

A _____ is a type of window used to modify a group of settings or enter information. In Windows, a dialog box displays whenever additional information is needed. A dialog box can contain option buttons, sliders, tabs, drop-down list boxes, and check boxes.

*   An _____ allows you to select only one of several options.
    You click an option button to select it. When an option button is selected, it contains a black dot.

*   A _____ allows you to change values by dragging it left or right. On each side of a slider are opposing values, such as Slow and Fast or High and Low.

*   A _____ allows you to move through groups of options in a dialog box.
    To display a different sheet of options, you click the tab.

- A _____ looks like a white box with some text and a down-arrow button. When you click the down-arrow button, a list of choices displays. The current selection is highlighted in the drop-down list. As soon as a new item is clicked, the list diappears and the selected item appears in the drop-down list box.

- A _____ is used to select more than one option. You click a check box to select it. When a check box is selected, it contains a check mark. You can select only one option button in an area, but you can select multiple check boxes.

Dialog boxes also may contain text boxes, where text is displayed or entered, and spin boxes, which are used to scroll though values in set increments.

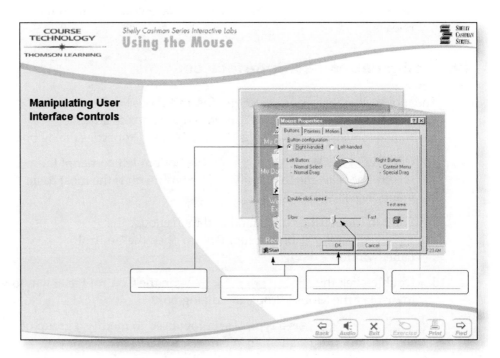

Figure 1

Evaluating the Results

True/False

Instructions: Circle T if the statement is true or F if the statement is false.

T F 1. When the mouse pointer is pointing to an object on the screen and then one of the mouse buttons is pressed, it is called dragging the object.

T F 2. To double-click an object, point to it with the mouse pointer and then press both mouse buttons at the same time.

T F 3. When dragging an object, the object is dropped as soon as the mouse button is released.

T F 4. A check box is turned on or off by clicking it.

T F 5. Clicking the down arrow in a list box scrolls through the options in that list.

Matching

Instructions: Write the letter of a description from the column on the right in front of each term in the column on the left.

_____ 1. Check boxes

_____ 2. Option buttons

_____ 3. Drop-down list boxes

_____ 4. Sliders

_____ 5. Dialog boxes

a. may contain several user interface controls

b. look like white boxes with some text next to a down arrow

c. are rectangular areas in which text is typed

d. act like switches to turn alternatives on or off

e. form a group of choices from which only one can be selected

f. immediately execute an action or command

g. can be dragged to set a value within a range

Using the Mouse

Multiple Choice

Instructions: Circle the correct response.

1. What is mouse used for in a graphical user interface?
   a. to enter text into the computer
   b. to select options and move items on the screen
   c. to convert information on paper into digital information a computer can use
   d. to store a large number of programs and data

2. In what direction does the mouse pointer on the screen move if the mouse is moved forward (in the direction of the cable by which it is attached to the computer)?
   a. up
   b. down
   c. left
   d. right

3. What should you do if you run out of desk space while moving the mouse?
   a. slide the mouse back to its starting point and try moving it again
   b. double-click the mouse button then slide the mouse in the opposite direction
   c. move the mouse more slowly across the desk top
   d. lift the mouse off the desk top and reposition it in the center of the area

4. What mouse operation is used frequently to open a file or begin running an application?
   a. pointing
   b. clicking
   c. double-clicking
   d. dragging

5. Which of the following are used to select one option out of several in a group?
   a. option buttons
   b. check boxes
   c. sliders
   d. scroll bars

Fill in the Blanks

Instructions: Place the correct word(s) in the blank in each sentence.

1. A(n) _____ is a unique pointing device that fits in the palm of your hand.

2. Moving the mouse across a mousepad or the top of a desk controls the movement of a(n) _____ (arrow) on the screen.

3. To select objects such as menu commands and buttons, you _____ them.

4. In a graphical user interface, _____ often is used to move objects.

5. _____ an object displays a shortcut menu related to that object.

Examining the Issues

1. Although the mouse was first invented in the early 1970s, its popularity grew slowly until the introduction of the Apple Macintosh computer in 1984. The Macintosh had a graphical user interface and was sold with a mouse. Today, the mouse is an almost essential input device for all personal computers; many software packages require the use of a mouse. Will the mouse still be popular thirty years from now, or will it be replaced by a different type of pointing device? Why? What factors could make another pointing device, such as a joystick or trackball, more popular than the mouse?

2. Before the advent of the graphical user interface, people had to type commands to instruct the computer to perform various tasks. For example, to delete a file named Charlie, a user would type the command, del Charlie. This method of communicating with the computer is called a command-driven interface. With a graphical user interface, however, an operator may use the mouse to drag an icon representing Charlie over an icon picturing a trash can to perform the same task. What are the advantages of using a GUI? What are the disadvantages?

Investigating the World

1. Originally, the computer mouse had a simple rectangular shape, something like a deck of cards. Today, a mouse can come in a variety of shapes and sizes and even have different numbers and types of buttons, including wheels. Using catalogs, brochures, or trade magazines, obtain pictures of at least five different mouse types. What are the advantages of each? What are the disadvantages? If you were going to purchase one for your personal computer, which would you buy? Why?

2. Instead of a mouse, some computers use other pointing devices such as trackballs or joysticks. Visit a computer vendor and find a computer that uses a pointing device other than the mouse. What kind of computer is it? What type of pointing device does it use? Why? Try using this device to maneuver the mouse pointer. Would you buy a computer with this type of pointing device? Why or why not?

Using the Keyboard

Summarizing the Lab

2

Instructions: Use the Using the Keyboard interactive lab to complete the following outline.

I. What is a keyboard?

A keyboard is an input device that allows you to _____ with a computer.

The keyboard is the most commonly used input device. Unlike the mouse, however, training is required to use the keyboard efficiently. Although all computer keyboards may seem alike, the keys on the keyboard, the placement of keys, the spaces between the keys, the feel of the keys, and the noise produced when a key is pressed may vary. As a result, operators sometimes feel that one keyboard is easier to use than another.

The keyboard is used to enter _____ , _____ , and _____ .

Recently, some keyboards have been designed ergonomically in an effort to minimize repetitive strain injuries such as carpal tunnel syndrome (CTS). These keyboards may use wrist rests and alternative key layouts that the manufacturers claim keep an operator's hands in more natural positions.

II. Elements of the keyboard

Five categories of keys on the keyboard are shown in Figure 2 on the next page.

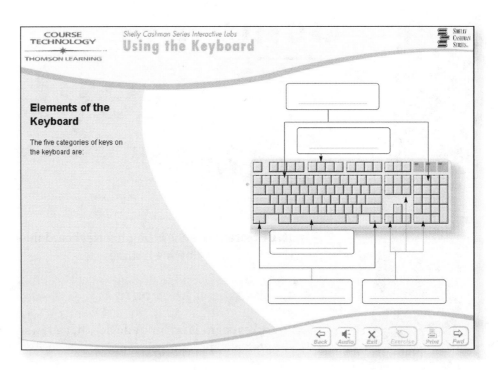

COURSE
TECHNOLOGY

THOMSON LEARNING

Shelly Cashman Series Interactive Labs
Using the Keyboard

SHELLY
CASHMAN
SERIES.

Elements of the Keyboard

The five categories of keys on the keyboard are:

Figure 2

The position of the function keys, navigation keys, and numeric keypad may vary depending on the keyboard's age and manufacturer. The original 83-key IBM keyboard placed the function keys in two columns on the left side of the keyboard. The keyboard shown in this lab is representative of the 101-key enhanced IBM compatible keyboard.

At the top right corner of the keyboard there are also _____ .

When the computer is turned on (booted) it checks the keyboard. On many computers, the status lights flash while this check is taking place.

Exploring Your Computer

Is your computer keyboard a 101-key IBM compatible keyboard? Is it a larger keyboard or a smaller, portable-style keyboard? Are there status lights for NUM LOCK, CAPS LOCK, and SCROLL LOCK? Right now, are any of these lights on? Does your keyboard have a numeric keypad? How is your keyboard different from the one shown in this lab?

A. The _____ are similar to those on a standard type-writer.

A modification of the conventional keyboard is available with Braille key-caps for the visually impaired. Keyboards with alternative alphabetic key layouts also are available.

There are three types of alphabetic keys: _____ , _____ , and _____ .

Some keys may represent more than one function. Alphabetic keys enter lowercase letters when the key alone is pressed, or uppercase letters if the _____ key is held down while the key is pressed or if the _____ key is pressed.

The _____ shows that the alphabetic keys will transmit uppercase letters rather than lowercase letters.

The **CAPS LOCK** key is called a toggle key because it turns on a mode when pressed and turns off the mode when pressed again. The **NUM LOCK** key and, in some software applications, the **INSERT** (**INS**) key, are also toggle keys. Unlike the **SHIFT** key, the **CAPS LOCK** key cannot be used to print the top character shown on keys with two characters (such as the key with 1 and !).

B. The _____ contains keys similar to those on an adding machine or calculator.

To use these keys, it is necessary to press the _____ key in the top left corner of the keypad.

When the _____ is lit, the keys in the numeric keypad perform like those on a calculator.

The numeric keypad is designed for rapid entry of numeric data. Due to space limitations, portable computers (notebooks, subnotebooks, and laptops) usually do not have numeric keypads.

C. _____ include arrow keys and four special keys that can be used to move through text on the screen.

An insertion point, or cursor, is a symbol that indicates where on the screen the next character typed will appear.

When the _____ key is turned off, some of the keys on the numeric keypad can be used to move the insertion point. There are dedicated arrow keys as well.

When an arrow key is pressed, the cursor moves one space in the same direction as the arrow on the key. Holding down an arrow key moves the insertion point rapidly in the indicated direction.

Four other keys can be used to navigate on the screen: _____ , _____ , _____ , and _____ . The functions of these keys change depending on the software application.

D. The _____ along the top of the keyboard are used to accomplish certain tasks quickly.

Function keys are used mostly to transmit _____ to the computer.

Some software applications provide keyboard templates, which are plastic sheets designed to fit on the keyboard next to the function keys. They indicate the command each key performs.

Function keys can be _____ for specific tasks.

Because of this capability, function keys also are called programmable keys, or soft keys, because their functions usually are assigned by the software package.

Some function keys have fixed meanings; other function keys mean different things depending on the software application being used. Software manufacturers have tried to standardize the purpose of a few function keys. For example, function key **F1** often can be used to obtain Help on an application.

Knowledge of the uses of function keys can save a computer operator a great deal of time. Windows applications, however, generally depend more on using icons and a pointing device than on function keys.

Exploring Windows

The Microsoft Natural keyboard includes three new keys that are not part of traditional computer keyboards. These keys and special key combinations trigger actions that are specifically for Microsoft's Windows operating system. Some of these actions include accessing the Start menu, activating taskbar buttons, displaying the Run dialog box, and minimizing documents.

E. Depending on the application being used, the _____ perform specific tasks more efficiently.

How special keys are used:

1. The _____ key generally is used to exit from a dialog box or an application.

2. The _____ and _____ keys may turn the alphabetic keys into function keys or may change their meanings in other ways.

Usually, the **CTRL** key makes a key perform a _____ function.

Usually, the **ALT** key gives the key an _____ meaning.

The **CTRL** and **ALT** keys are used like the _____ key — by holding down the **CTRL** or **ALT** key while pressing another key on the keyboard.

Special keys that usually are used alone include **ENTER** (enters data or completes a paragraph), **BACKSPACE** (erases the character just typed), **TAB** (advances the insertion point to a defined spot), **DELETE** (erases the character to the right of the insertion point), **INSERT** (allows a character to be inserted or toggles insert typing mode on and off), and **PRINT SCREEN** (prints the current screen display or stores it in the computer's memory).

Special key combinations in the Windows environment perform specific tasks:

- _____ displays the list of applications that are open.

- Pressing _____ while holding down the **ALT** key displays the name of the next open application one by one.

In the Windows environment, special keys may be used in combination with the mouse. For example, holding down the **CTRL** key while clicking the mouse button sometimes can be used to select more than one item.

Exploring Online

Many keyboard-related sites exist on the Internet. For example, the Computer Museum in Boston has a home page that shows how a giant keyboard was built as part of its Walk-Through Computer exhibit.

The Keyboard Alternatives Web site provides keyboard descriptions, graphics, and advice that can help in choosing the best keyboard for various needs. For more information on using a keyboard, visit the Exploring Computers Web page (www.scsite.com/expl.htm) and click Keyboards.

Evaluating Results
the

True/False

Instructions: Circle **T** if the statement is true or **F** if the statement is false.

T F 1. Each of the many keys on a keyboard can represent only one function.

T F 2. When the Num Lock light is lit, some of the keys on the numeric keypad can be used to control the insertion point

T F 3. In general, the **HOME** key moves the insertion point to the beginning of a document.

T F 4. Exactly what tasks the special keys on the keyboard perform depends largely on the software being used.

T F 5. Usually, the **CTRL** key makes a key perform a control function, such as a command.

Matching

Instructions: Write the letter of a description from the column on the right in front of each term in the column on the left.

____ 1. Alphabetic keys

____ 2. Numeric keys

____ 3. Navigation keys

____ 4. Function keys

____ 5. Special keys

a. perform specific tasks more efficiently

b. are similar to those on a standard typewriter

c. include arrow keys and four special keys

d. are used to turn the computer on and off

e. are similar to those on an adding machine or calculator

f. are used mostly to transmit commands to the computer

g. show the status of each toggle key

Multiple Choice

Instructions: Circle the correct response.

1. Where are the status lights located on the keyboard?
   a. upper right corner
   b. lower right corner
   c. upper left corner
   d. lower left corner

2. Which of the following is not a type of alphabetic key?
   a. a letter key
   b. a punctuation key
   c. the **SPACE BAR**
   d. a navigation key

3. What type of keys can be programmed for specific tasks?
   a. alphabetic keys
   b. numeric keys
   c. function keys
   d. special keys

4. How are the **SHIFT**, **CTRL**, and **ALT** keys used with other keys?
   a. press a key and release it, then press the **SHIFT**, **CTRL**, or **ALT** key
   b. press a key and hold it down, then press the **SHIFT**, **CTRL**, or **ALT** key
   c. hold down the **SHIFT**, **CTRL**, or **ALT** key while pressing another key
   d. quickly press the **SHIFT**, **CTRL**, or **ALT** key simultaneously with another key

5. In the Windows environment, pressing what key combination displays the list of open programs?
   a. **CTRL+ESC**
   b. **ALT+TAB**
   c. **CTRL+TAB**
   d. **ALT+ESC**

Using the
Keyboard

Fill in the Blanks

Instructions: Place the correct word(s) in the blank in each sentence.

1. The _____ light indicates that the alphabetic keys will now transmit uppercase letters instead of lowercase letters.

2. To use the numeric keypad, it is necessary first to press the _____ key on the numeric keypad.

3. In general, the _____ key moves up one screen.

4. The _____ keys along the top of the keyboard are used to accomplish certain tasks quickly.

5. The _____ key generally is used to exit from a dialog box or an application.

Examining the Issues

1. The traditional arrangement of letters on the keyboard is called the QWERTY layout, a name that comes from the first six keys on the top row of letters. This layout, designed by Christopher Sholes in the 1800s, was developed to slow down typists and prevent the keys from jamming. Although having keys jam is no longer a problem, most keyboards today continue to use the same arrangement of letters. Yet, alternative designs are available. The Dvorak keyboard places the most commonly typed letters in the home row, or the row on which the fingers rest. The Maltron keyboard is split and shaped to fit each hand, with the most commonly used keys under the strongest fingers. What are the advantages of the Dvorak and Maltron layouts? What are the disadvantages? On which keyboard would a trained typist be able to enter the fastest input? Why? Will the Dvorak or Maltron layouts ever be widely accepted? Why or why not?

2. You can enter numbers into a computer by using either the numeric keypad or the row of numbers above the alphabetic keys. Under what circumstances would you be more likely to use the numeric keypad to enter numbers? Why? When would you be more likely to use the row of numbers above the alphabetic keys? Why?

Investigating the World

1. In 2000, sales of portable computers (laptop, notebook, and subnotebook) constituted almost 35 percent of total computer sales. Portable computers have the same capabilities as many desktop personal computers. Many components have been miniaturized for use in portable computers, but because the keys must be large enough to accommodate human fingers it is difficult to downsize the keyboard. A common approach taken by manufacturers has been to use fewer keys and carry out certain tasks by pressing two or more keys simultaneously. Visit a computer vendor and try two portable computers. What keys described in this lab have been eliminated on each portable computer keyboard? How are the tasks performed by these keys accomplished on each portable computer? Which portable computer is easier to use? Why?

2. Computer keyboards for some non-European based languages can be considerably more complex than the keyboards with which we are familiar. Different alphabets pose special problems for keyboard designers. For example, most Japanese writing is a combination of kanji (1,850 basic characters) and kana (additional symbols representing specific syllables), far more symbols than on our standard keyboards! Visit a library or other research facility to learn about computer keyboards used with a non-European based language. What problems for keyboard designers, if any, are suggested by the language's alphabet? How have the problems been addressed? What symbols are used on the keyboard? How are the non-alphabetic keys (navigation keys, function keys, numeric keys, and special keys) different from those on our standard keyboard?

Connecting to the Internet

Summarizing the Lab

3

Instructions: Use the Connecting to the Internet interactive lab to complete the following outline.

I. What is the Internet?

The Internet (also called the Net) is a _____ of computer networks that links people, educational institutions, government agencies, and businesses.

A network uses communications channels to share data, information, hardware, and software among connected computers. The Internet is composed of INTERconnected NETworks. Begun in 1969 as a way for government computers to communicate with each other, the Internet expanded to include universities and private research sites. In the early 1990s, new software called web browsers simplified access for people outside the scientific and academic communities. Today, the Internet has more than 100 million users located in 200 countries, 100,000 connected networks, and 12 million host computers or sites. Since 1988, the Internet has doubled in size — and it continues to grow explosively each year.

II. Communicating over the Internet

The more common Internet services available are:
_____ , _____ , _____ , _____ , and _____ .

A. Using _____ , or _____ , is much like writing a letter. Message files are created, addressed, and sent to the recipient's e-mail address.

Electronic mail is the most widely used service on the Internet. When a message arrives, it is stored in a special file, called the mail box, on the destination computer using the recipient's account name as the file name. After issuing a command to read incoming mail, the recipient can save, delete, reply to, or otherwise manage the message.

The standard format for an e-mail address is:

_____ @ _____ . _____

1. _____ is the person's e-mail account name.

   Usernames must be unique to the domain. They often consist of a first initial and last name. Because spaces are not allowed in usernames, underscores may be substituted (for example, john_smith@ibm.com).

2. _____ is the location where the user's account is set up.

   The domain can be more than one word, separated by periods or dots (for example, jsmith@finance.ibm.com). This might happen when the account is set up on a local area network (LAN) that is part of an organization with several different LANs.

3. _____ is an abbreviation for the kind of organization where the account is located.

   There are a number of top-level domain types. In addition to com (commercial organizations), edu (educational organiza-tions), and org (other organizations), some other types are mil (US military groups), gov (US government institutions), int (interna-tional organizations) and net (network resources).

Informal rules, called e-mail etiquette or netiquette, have been developed for using e-mail. These rules include keeping messages short and distribution lists to a minimum, avoiding gossip, respecting the confidentiality of others, and not engaging in flaming, or sending rude, inflammatory messages.

Because e-mail messages are read without benefit of hearing the sender's tone of voice or seeing any facial expression, senders sometimes include symbols to convey their mood. To interpret these symbols, often called smileys, a reader rotates the page 90° clockwise. Common smileys include — :) (smile), : ((frown), ;) (wink), : I (indifference), and : D (laugh out loud).

B. _____ , or

   _____ , is a way to send and receive files over the Internet.

   Using FTP software, users can connect to certain computers on the Internet called _____ . These computers act as FTP sites that send users the file they request.

   Archie is special software that can be used to search for specific files. Archie returns the Internet address of the files located, and FTP then can be used to retrieve them.

   Files on FTP sites often are compressed to save downloading time, in which case a program like PKZIP or WINZIP is needed to extract the compressed file.

Exploring Online

Several search tools and directories are available to assist in navigating the Internet. Examples include Yahoo!, Lycos, Excite, Hotbot, and WebCrawler. You can access one of these World Wide Web sites and perform a search for a topic that interests you, such as a favorite sports team, music group, or TV program. For more details about using search tools on the Internet, visit the Exploring Computers Web page (www.scsite.com/expl.htm) and click Internet.

C. _____ are message areas where people can discuss a common area of interest.

Newsgroups are available on almost any subject, including such diverse topics as vendor products, recipes, gardening, music, and more. A newsgroup name, such as rec.sport.golf, begins with a category name and is followed by one or more words that narrow down the main topic of the group. Category names include: comp (computer topics), talk (discussion), alt (alternative discussions), biz (business), info (information), misc (miscellaneous topics), rec (recreational topics), and sci (scientific topics).

In some newsgroups, before posting an article a moderator reviews it to determine if it is relevant to the discussion. Because this ensures that articles are appropriate, the content of a moderated newsgroup often is considered more valuable.

Usenet is an informal group of systems that exchange news on a variety of topics. An article posted to a newsgroup on one system is duplicated throughout Usenet, with each participating computer site eventually receiving a copy.

D. A _____ is a real-time typed conversation that takes place on a computer. A _____ is a location on an Internet server that permits real-time conversations.

Like newsgroups, chat rooms usually are specific to a certain topic. As you type on your keyboard, however, everyone connected to the same chat room server sees the typed characters. This real-time character of chat makes chat rooms different from newsgroups. Some chat rooms support voice chats and video chats, so you can hear or see other chat room participants. The person who creates a chat room usually is responsible for monitoring conversations and disconnecting anyone who is disruptive. In some chat rooms, particularly those aimed at adults, a monitor's presence hardlly is noticed. Chat rooms intended for minors, however, often are closely monitored.

_____ is another real-time communications service that allows people to exchange messages or files.

Many instant messaging (IM) services also can alert you to information such as calendar appointments, stock quotes, weather forecasts, or sports scores.

E.   The _____ is a vast collection of hyperlinked documents, called Web pages, containing images, sounds, and even video. This collection is stored in computer systems around the world called _____ . Web pages are viewed using a _____ .

The World Wide Web combines e-mail, FTP, and newsgroups. Using hypertext links, related information is grouped together for easy retrieval. Clicking a link (also called a hyperlink) on a Web page leads to other text files, graphics, sounds, or video.

Web browsers have a graphical interface that can be used to look at multimedia documents on host computers around the world. Surfing is a slang term for browsing the Internet.

A _____ is a World Wide Web site designed to offer a variety of Internet services from a single location.

III. Gaining access to the Internet

> ### Exploring Windows
> Windows comes with software that links users to The Microsoft Network (MSN), an online service offered by Microsoft that provides access to the Internet. Microsoft also offers software for connecting to the Internet and a World Wide Web browser in the Microsoft Plus! software package.

Employees of a company connected to the Internet and students at most secondary schools are able to take advantage of the Internet. Home users can access the Internet by subscribing to a _____ .

Fees for service providers vary greatly. Some have a higher fixed monthly charge with a low hourly connect-time fee. Others have a lower fixed monthly charge and a higher hourly connect-time fee.

During normal business hours, some public libraries and local governments offer limited public Internet access.

IV. Connecting to the Internet from home

To access an Internet service, you can use a _____ , to dial over regular telephone lines. This is the slowest, but least expensive, connection option.

Exploring Your Computer

Is your computer connected to the Internet? If so, are you connected directly to the Internet through a network, or do you dial into it through a modem? What Internet services described in this lab are you able to use?

The word modem is a combination of the words modulate (to change a computer's digital signal into a sound or analog signal) and demodulate (to convert an analog signal into a digital signal). Dialing software stores, selects, and dials telephone numbers of computers that can be called.

Two types of Internet connections are:

A. With _____ service, the computer and modem are used to connect to another computer attached to the Internet. Mail, news, and other programs are then run on the _____ .

B. A _____ (Serial Line Internet Protocol) or _____ (Point to Point Protocol) account enables a computer to communicate over telephone lines with a group of networked computers. With SLIP or PPP, all information is sent directly to _____ .

V. Structure of the Internet

Devices that play a role in getting a message across the Internet include those illustrated in Figure 11 on the next page.

A. When a user sends a message using a PC at home, the message first is sent over telephone lines to the _____ that handles the user's account.

B. When the message arrives, the _____ determines where the message should go.

   The server is a computer dedicated to handling the communication needs of the other computers in the network.

C. If the message is to be sent to another network, the server sends it to a _____ , which sends messages between networks using a variety of communications channels. These may include telephone lines or fiber-optic cables, microwaves, or satellite transmissions.

   A router is an intelligent network-connecting device that can route communications directly to the appropriate network.

D. When the message reaches its destination network, a router passes it to the _____ . The message is transferred to the _____ , which stores it in the recipient's personal electronic mail box.

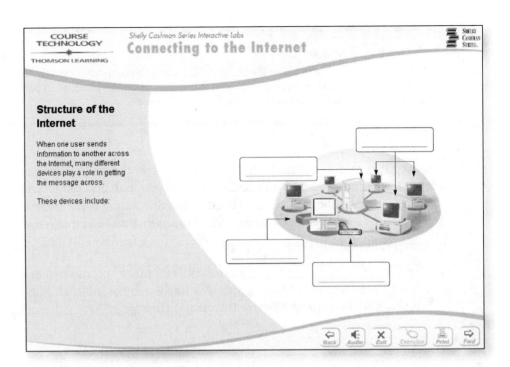

COURSE
TECHNOLOGY

THOMSON LEARNING

Shelly Cashman Series Interactive Labs

Connecting to the Internet

SHELLY
CASHMAN
SERIES.

**Structure of the
Internet**

When one user sends
information to another across
the Internet, many different
devices play a role in getting
the message across.

These devices include:

Back Audio Exit Exercise Print Fwd

Figure 3

A gateway is a combination of hardware and software that allows users
on one network to access the resources on a different network.

E. When the user connects to the network, the server transfers the
    message to his or her personal computer.

Evaluating **Results**
the

True/False

Instructions: Circle **T** if the statement is true or **F** if the statement is false.

T F 1. The Internet is a vast network of computer networks that links millions of people and thousands of educational institutions and corporations world wide.

T F 2. Newsgroups are similar to traditional broadcast news in that people can read the contents of the group but cannot contribute to it.

T F 3. Hyperlinked documents that contain images, sound, and even video are known as Web sites.

T F 4. When your computer is connected to the Internet using a remote log-in service, all information from any e-mail or news programs run is sent directly to your computer.

T F 5. Devices that play a role when one user sends information to another across the Internet include network servers, network routers, computer workstations, and modems.

Matching

Instructions: Write the letter of a description from the column on the right in front of each term in the column on the left.

_____ 1. FTP

_____ 2. chat room

_____ 3. newsgroup

_____ 4. instant messaging

_____ 5. World Wide Web

a. a program used to display information about another's computer account

b. the entire collection of hyperlinked documents stored in computer systems around the world

c. real-time communications service that allows people to exchange messages or files

d. a search tool that helps to locate and retrieve documents on the Internet

e. message area where people can post and read messages about a common area of interest

f. location on an Internet server that permits real-time conversations

g. a way to send and receive files over the Internet

Connecting to the
Internet

Multiple Choice

Instructions: Circle the correct response.

1. What is the standard format for an e-mail address?
    a. username.type@domain
    b. domain@type.username
    c. type.username@domain
    d. username@domain.type

2. What is the com extension short for in an e-mail address?
    a. community group
    b. commercial organization
    c. communications personnel
    d. communist party

3. What are two widely used Web browsers?
    a. Microsoft PowerPoint and Corel Presentations
    b. Microsoft Internet Explorer and Netscape Navigator
    c. Microsoft Outlook and Lotus Organizer
    d. Microsoft Pocket Excel and Corel Quattro Pro

4. What is the slowest, but least expensive, way to connect to the Internet?
    a. use a modem to dial over a regular telephone line
    b. use an ISDN adapter connected to a dedicated ISDN line
    c. use a special DSL model to access DSL
    d. use a cable modem to access cable service

5. What is the function of a network server?
    a. it determines where a message coming into the network should go
    b. it sends messages between networks using a variety of communications channels
    c. it receives all incoming messages and stores them in a mailbox
    d. it converts digital signals into analog signals that can travel over telephone lines

Fill in the Blanks

Instructions: Place the correct word(s) in the blank in each sentence.

1. Using _____ , a common Internet service, involves creating a text file, addressing the file, and sending it to the recipient's address.

2. Linkages between different documents, called _____ , may connect files anywhere in the world.

3. Web pages are viewed using a(n) _____ .

4. Home computer users can access the Internet by subscribing to a(n) _____ that offers connections to the Internet for a small monthly fee.

5. _____ send messages between networks using a variety of communications channels, such as telephone lines, microwaves, fiber-optic cable, and satellite transmissions.

Examining the Issues

1. The Internet has had a major impact on the way people use computers. Now, some companies are expecting the Internet to have an impact on the computers themselves. Several innovative manufacturers offer an alternative to the current PC called the NC, or network computer. The NC provides only the most-used functions: access to the Internet, word processing, e-mail, and video conferencing. Any additional software required can be downloaded from the Internet. NCs require fewer components and are about as powerful as the early 486 PCs, with a flat-panel monochrome display, keyboard, mouse, and modem. The NC does not have a hard drive, but relies instead on networks to handle any storage needs. Best of all, the NC sells for $500 – $1000. Is the NC the computer of the future, eventually replacing the PC? Why or why not? What problems might an NC user have?

2. Certain groups have suggested that dangerous information, along with material that is discriminatory, inflammatory, confidential, or obscene, should not be available on the Internet. They propose that controls be placed over the content of newsgroups, files, and documents on the Internet. Others maintain, however, that any restrictions threaten free speech. In addition, because the Internet is global in scope and standards for acceptable material vary from country to country, state to state, and even community to community, controls are unrealistic. Should controls be placed over the material available on the Internet? Why or why not?

Investigating the World

1. Most home users access the Internet through a service provider. Some of the more popular service providers are: America Online (800-827-6364), Prodigy (800-776-3449), CompuServe (800-848-8199), The Microsoft Network (800-386-5550), Delphi (800-695-4005), Netcom (800-NETCOM1), AT&T WorldNet (800-worldnet), and MCI Internet (800-550-0927). Call at least three of these service providers. What types of services do they offer? How is access to the Internet provided? Is a particular type of computer, operating system, modem, or interface required? What are the membership fees? Are there any other fees (such as an hourly access fee, minimum monthly charge, or added cost for certain services)? From the information you receive, in which service provider would you be most interested? Why?

2. One piece of computer hardware that can be used to access the Internet is a standard modem. Visit a computer vendor and compare several modems. List the characteristics of each, including such items as the transmission rate, the manufacturer, the cost, and whether it is an inter-nal or exter-nal modem. Consider the type of personal computer you already have, or would like to purchase, and how you would like to use the Internet. On the basis of the information you have gathered, which modem would you be most likely to purchase? Why?

The World Wide Web

Summarizing the Lab

4

Instructions: Use the *World Wide Web* interactive lab to complete the following outline.

I. What is the World Wide Web?

In 1991, a programmer developed a program that created documents, called _____ , with built-in links to other documents on the Internet. These links, called _____ , can be used to move quickly from one document to the next, no matter where the docu-ments are stored.

The collection of hyperlinked documents has become known as the

_____.

II. How does the World Wide Web work?

The Internet locations where Web pages are stored are _____. Multiple Web sites may exist on the same computer. Web sites are located on computers around the world that are connected to the _____. To view pages at these Web sites, a computer first must connect to the Internet.

III. Web pages

Web pages may contain several types of files, including text, graphics, animation, video, and executable programs. There are two types of Web pages:

- _____ link text documents to other text documents.

- _____ link text, video, graphics, and sound.

A. Web page links

A Web page can have three types of hyperlinks:

- _____ move from one location in a document to another location within the same document.

- _____ move from one document to another document on the same computer.

- _____ move to another document on a different computer.

Hyperlinks to other documents are displayed either as underlined text of a different color or as a graphic. When the mouse pointer is positioned over a hyperlink, the mouse pointer changes to a small hand with a pointing finger.

Hyperlinks make it possible to learn about subjects in a nonlinear manner. Reading a book from cover to cover — learning a subject in a straight line from beginning to end — is learning in a linear manner. Branching off and investigating related topics as they are encountered is a nonlinear way of learning. The ability to branch from one related topic to another makes hyperlinks a powerful tool and the Internet an interesting place to explore.

Jumping from one Web page to another is called _____.

B. Creating a Web page

Web pages are created using _____, which are special codes that define how a page will look and specify the links to other documents.

Once these special instructions, called _____, are added to a document and the document is saved as HTML, it can be viewed as a Web page using a Web browser.

HTML tags, or markups, can be generated by using Web page authoring software specifically designed for this task, or by using Web page authoring features included in many word processing and desktop publishing applications.

Exploring Online

Many Web sites, such as Newbie Help, provide a welcome resource for those new to the Internet and the Web (otherwise known as newbies). After you have mastered the basics, you can learn how to build your own Web page by visiting pages such as The NCSA Beginner's Guide to HTML and A Basic Home Page, which teach the basics of hypertext markup language (HTML) and Web page design. For more details on basic World Wide Web concepts, visit the Exploring Computers Web page (www.scsite.com/expl.htm) and click World Wide Web.

IV. Web browser software

A _____ is a program that displays Web pages and allows users to link to other Web pages.

The first Web browsers used text commands and displayed only text documents. In 1993, however, Mark Andreesen created a Web browser called Mosaic that displayed documents with graphics and used a graphical interface. Mosaic contributed to the rapid growth of the Internet by making it easier and more enjoyable to view Web documents. Andreesen later became one of the founders of Netscape Communications Corpora-tion, a leading Internet software company.

Two of the more common Web browsers are Microsoft Internet Explorer and Netscape Navigator. To view Web pages, a Web browser connects to an Internet computer through an Internet access provider.

The more frequently used Web browser features that are available on the toolbar include:

- _____
- _____
- _____
- _____
- _____
- _____
- _____

A. Each time a Web browser is launched, a Web page called a _____ is retrieved and displayed. This page typically is the Web page of the Internet access provider or the manufacturer of the browser.

Although the term, home page, often is used to describe the first page at a Web site, the first page technically is called the Welcome page.

The Web browser home page often provides a quick way to learn about Internet services, new utilities or services, or Internet related news.

Exploring Windows

Microsoft uses the World Wide Web to provide regular updates to the Windows operating system. These updates are files that add various functions and features to the operating system, such as device drivers, support tools, mini-applications, utilities, toys, and more. The Windows updates are available free from the Microsoft software library on the Web. After you are connected to the Internet, you can browse through the Windows updates and download files to your computer.

B. A Web page is retrieved using a

_____ , which is an address of a

Web page on the Internet.

A URL can specify a:

- _____

- _____

- _____

The URL displays in the address box of the Web browser. All Web page URLs begin with _____ (hypertext transfer protocol), the communications standard for transferring pages on the Web.

The basic elements of a URL are shown in Figure 4.

COURSE TECHNOLOGY

THOMSON LEARNING

Shelly Cashman Series Interactive Labs

The World Wide Web

SHELLY CASHMAN SERIES.

How a Web Browser Works

Uniform Resource Locator (URL)

The basic elements of a URL are:

http://www.scseries.com/scseries/scseries.html#default

Figure 4

Some browsers display the URL of a hyperlinked document at the bottom of the screen. The document can be displayed by clicking the hyperlink or typing the URL in the Location text box of the Web browser. Some browsers change the color of a text hyperlink after it is clicked.

C. Web page URLs can be stored in a favorites or bookmark list. A bookmark consists of the title of a Web page and the URL of that page. A Web page can be retrieved by clicking the _____ button and then simply selecting it from the list.

D. A Web browser keeps track of the Web pages viewed from the moment the browser is launched to when it is exited. The _____ can be used to revisit pages that have been viewed. Web pages also can be printed directly from the Web browser using the _____.

> ### Exploring Your Computer
> Does your computer have a Web browser? If so, which one? Is it the latest version of that particular browser? Have you created any bookmarks in your Bookmarks or Favorites list? Is the Exploring Computers Web page in your bookmarks list?

E. The _____ interrupts the loading of a Web page. The _____ is used to reload a Web page from its Web site. The Refresh button might be used with pages that update frequently or to continue loading a Web page after the Stop button has been clicked.

F. Because the Web contains thousands of Web sites on a wide variety of topics, finding information on a specific subject can be difficult. Several companies have created sites with organized directories of Web pages and keyword search capabilities. The _____ displays some of the more popular search sites.

V. Search tools

A search tool, also called a _____ , is a program that finds Web sites, Web pages, and Internet files that match keywords. Some search tools look for simple word matches and others allow for more specific searches on a series of words or an entire phrase. The search engine searches an index of Internet sites and documents that is constantly being revised and updated.

The two general types of search tools are:

• _____ that organize related Web resources by type.

• _____ search programs that find Web pages and files that match specified key words.

Most search sites with directories organize Web pages into categories such as sports, entertainment, or business.

Some popular search tools are Yahoo!, Infoseek, Lycos, AltaVista, Excite, WebCrawler, Four11, and BigBook.

Evaluating the Results

True/False

Instructions: Circle **T** if the statement is true or **F** if the statement is false.

T F 1. The World Wide Web is a collection of documents at various locations, called Web sites, all over the world.

T F 2. Hypertext documents link text, video, graphics, and sound.

T F 3. Web pages are created using hypertext markup language (HTML).

T F 4. A Web page is retrieved using a Uniform Resource Locator, or URL.

T F 5. All Web page URLs begin with WWW, which stands for World Wide Web, the communications standard for transferring pages on the Web.

Matching

Instructions: Write the letter of a description from the column on the right in front of each term in the column on the left.

____ 1. Forward and Back buttons

____ 2. Stop button

____ 3. Refresh button

____ 4. Home button

____ 5. Favorites button

a. retrieves a designated opening page

b. stores locations of preferred pages

c. displays tools for searching the Web

d. reloads the current Web page

e. interrupts a transmission

f. prints all or a portion of a Web page

g. moves through viewed pages

Multiple Choice

Instructions: Circle the correct response.

1. What type of hyperlink moves from one location in a document to another location within the same document?
   a. target hyperlink
   b. relative hyperlink
   c. absolute hyperlink
   d. all of the above

2. What are the special HTML codes that define how a Web page will look?
   a. tags
   b. links
   c. engines
   d. keywords

3. What can be specified by a URL?
   a. a Web site
   b. a document on a Web site
   c. a part of a document on a Web site
   d. all of the above

4. What function is performed by the domain name in a URL?
   a. it specifies the communications standard
   b. it references a specific part of a long document
   c. it identifies the computer that stores the Web page
   d. it is the name of the Web page

5. Which button on the toolbar of a Web browser displays many popular tools used to locate information?
   a. Search
   b. Favorites
   c. Home
   d. Refresh

Fill in the Blanks

Instructions: Place the correct word(s) in the blank in each sentence.

1. Web page links are called _____ because they are used to move quickly from one document to another on various Web sites.

2. Jumping from one Web page to another is called _____.

3. A(n) _____ is a program that displays Web pages and allows you to link to other Web pages.

4. A(n) _____ is a program that locates Web sites.

5. One general type of search tool is a(n) _____ , which organizes related Web resources by type.

Examining the Issues

1. Web advertisements are in basically two forms: a company's own Web site, or ad space on someone else's. Web advertising is expensive — the cost to reach 1,000 consumers with a thirty-second television spot is about $5.42, while the cost to reach 1,000 consumers with a one-month ad on an online magazine home page is about $75.00. Nevertheless, promoters point out two advantages to advertising on the Web:

   • Unlike a passive television audience, Web consumers make an effort to view an advertisement, actually clicking a hyperlink to visit a company's Web site.

   • Web users tend to be desirable consumers — students and highly educated individuals with median incomes of about $55,000.

   What type of products would benefit most from advertising on the Web? Why? How can advertisers encourage people to return to their Web site? Will Web advertising ever rival television, newspaper, or magazine advertisements? Why or why not?

2. In 1871, a Wells Fargo Wanted poster helped send Black Bart to prison for highway robbery. Once an adornment of bank and post office walls, Wanted posters today have found a new venue — the World Wide Web. Wells Fargo Bank has set up a Web site with small photographs of criminal suspects. Clicking one of the photo hyperlinks displays a larger picture, the reward offered (from $1,000 to $5,000), and a description of the crime. Some law enforcement agencies also are using the Web as a crime-fighting tool. The FBI has posted its 10 Most Wanted on a Web site since 1995. The success of these Web sites is not known, but one of the FBI's Internet posters may have led to the arrest of a bank robber in Guatemala when a 14-year old recognized the suspect as a family friend who helped him hook up his modem. What are the advantages of putting Wanted posters on Web sites? What are the disadvantages? How else might the Web be used to combat crime?

Investigating the World

1. Search engines constantly send out software *spiders* to canvas more than 80 million Web sites, reporting back information that is integrated into indexes. These indexes are combed whenever someone types in a keyword, and the results are displayed in seconds. Unfortunately, a typical query might return almost 50,000 replies. Although ranked by relevancy, locating the most suitable resource still can be cumbersome. A query about the nesting habits of cardinals may return sites having to do with Arizona's football team or prelates of the Catholic Church. Still, considering that the average Internet query is just over one word (queries from professional information seekers — academics and librarians — average about fourteen words), the success of search engines is remarkable. The engineering head of one search tool attributes this success to "wizardry and witchcraft." Think of a topic in which you are interested. Use two different search engines to find information about your topic. Which search engine worked better? Why? How were the returns similar? How were they different? What can a user do to make a search engine more effective?

2. For years, Netscape Navigator dominated Web browsers with a market share from 70 percent to 85 percent. Now, however, Microsoft's Internet Explorer is making its presence felt. By borrowing many of Netscape Navigator's features, being a part of the popular Windows operating system, and becoming the browser automatically supplied to America Online's 10 million users, Microsoft's Web browser has seized its own share of the browser market. Which browser is best? Talk to software vendors or users about at least two different Web browsers. How are they similar? How are they different? What are the advantages of each? If possible, try each browser and form your own opinion on their relative merits. Which Web browser would you be more likely to buy? Why?

Word Processing

Summarizing the Lab

5

Instructions: Use the Word Processing interactive lab to complete the following outline.

I. Word processing software

Word processing is the ability to produce or modify text to create a document.

Word processing software enables the computer to generate both a _____ and an _____ of a document.

II. Word processing documents

Word processing software is used to produce:

- _____   - _____   - _____
- _____   - _____   - _____

III. Capabilities of word processing software

Documents are stored _____ , so they can be retrieved and edited quickly.

Words, sentences, or entire sections can be added, deleted, or rearranged without having to retype the entire document.

IV. Producing a document

Producing a document involves the steps described in Figure 5 on the next page.

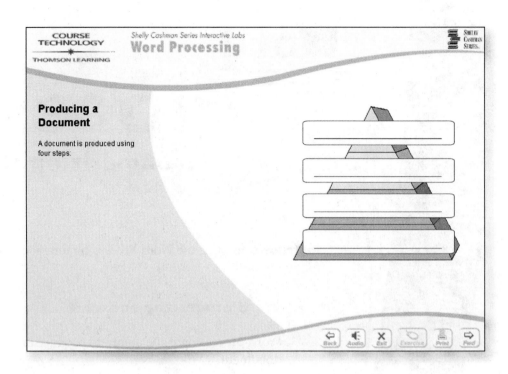

Producing a Document

A document is produced using four steps:

Back   Audio   Exit   Exercise   Print   Fwd

Figure 5

A. Creating a document

1. _____ enters an automatic line return when the text reaches a certain position in the document.

2. A document can be viewed as one continuous piece of paper or broken up into pages.

    _____ is the process of moving through a document to view its various parts.

    Clicking the scroll arrows on the scroll bars shifts the document up and down or right and left.

3. The insertion point indicates where the next character will appear on the screen.

    The insertion point can be moved with a pointing device by _____ where text should be added.

    The _____ on the keyboard move the insertion point one character or line at a time. When the arrow keys are held down, the movement is repeated until the key is released.

    The _____ and _____ keys move the insertion point a full screen.

    The _____ and _____ keys move the insertion point to the beginning or end of a line.

B. Editing a document

Exploring Windows

Windows includes two applications that allow users to create simple word processing documents: Notepad and WordPad. Notepad has a very basic window with an area for text entry, a title bar, and a menu bar. All documents created in Notepad are saved as text files. Unlike Notepad, the WordPad window includes a title bar, a menu bar, *and* toolbars with buttons such as Save, Print, Copy, and Paste. WordPad also allows you to format the text and save the document in several different file formats (including Word for Windows). To start either application, click the Start button, point to Programs on the Start menu, and point to Accessories on the submenu. Click Notepad or WordPad, depending on the application you wish to start.

1. _____ involves adding text to a document. _____ involves removing text.

    Insert mode automatically moves existing text to the right as new text is typed. Typeover mode replaces existing text as new text is typed. Most word processors normally are in insert mode.

    The _____ and _____ keys provide a simple way to remove text.

    The DELETE key removes characters to the right of the insertion point, and the BACKSPACE key removes characters to the left.

2. Cutting removes selected text from a document and stores it electronically on a location called the _____ .

    _____ duplicates selected text on the Clipboard so it can be pasted somewhere else.

    You can use _____ menus to cut or copy selected text and then paste it in another location.

3. Drag-and-drop editing involves moving a part of a document by dragging it from one position and dropping it in another.

4. The_____ feature finds all occurrences of a character, word, or group of words. The _____ feature is used to replace characters or words with a new character, word, or group of words.

Some word processors also can find specific formats, use wildcards, and even locate words that sound like other words.

5. A _____ reviews words, sections, or entire documents for correct spelling.

Some spell checkers review text as it is entered, marking words that might be misspelled.

A _____ is used to look up synonyms for words in a document.

_____ review grammar and check writing style and sentence structure. Most grammar checkers let users apply different rules for different types of writing (such as casual, formal, or technical).

6. New word processing programs are being geared for _____ editing.

Online editing circulates an electronic version of a document over a network, allowing people to suggest corrections or changes before a final copy of the document is printed. Often, a different color is used for each reviewer.

_____ are used to flag additions and deletions.

_____ are used to add comments and edits to a document. _____ is used to emphasize essential parts of a document.

7. _____ is used to cancel an action from a list of recent actions performed in a document.

Exploring Your Computer

Do you have word processing software installed on your computer? If so, what is the name of the application? What templates are included with the software? Does it have features such as spell check, grammar checker, and a thesaurus? Does it support online editing? What types of graphics can you insert into a document? Does the word processor automatically save documents as you work on them?

C. Formatting a document

1. _____ is a specific set of characters that are designed the same.

Typefaces often are called _____. Font sizes are measured in _____.

A font is a specific combination of typeface and point size, such as 10-point Arial.

Common point sizes used in business correspondence are _____ points.

A point is approximately 1/72 of an inch high. 12 points is equivalent to 12/72, or 1/6, of an inch.

_____ is a feature that can be added to a font, such as bold, italics, or underlining.

2. Margins define the amount of empty space at the left, right, bottom and top of a document.

_____ is how text is positioned in relation to the right and left margins. The four common types of alignment are _____ , _____ , _____ , and _____ .

3. _____ is how far apart individual letters and lines of text are placed.

Monospacing uses the same amount of space for each character. Proportional spacing gives more space to wide characters (such as W) than to narrow characters (such as I).

_____ determines the distance from the bottom of one line to the bottom of the next line. The most common line spacings are _____ line spacing.

Some word processing software also allows exact line spacing to be specified, usually in points.

4. _____ arrange text like a newspaper or magazine. _____ organize text in rows and columns.

5. Most word processing programs are capable of including different types of graphics.

_____ usually comes in collections that are grouped by theme or description.

Pictures also can be taken with a _____ or converted into electronic form using a scanner.

Once a graphic is inserted into a document, it can be moved, resized, rotated, or cropped.

6. _____ accentuate text, graphics, or tables with a decorative line or box.

_____ darkens the background of an area to provide contrast.

Colors can be applied to graphics, borders, and shading. Unless a color printer is used, however, colors will print as shades of gray.

7. You can use cut and paste, or the _____ on the Insert menu, to place an object created with another application into a word processing document.

8. _____ is a useful feature with documents that have multiple pages.

   Text also can be placed at the top of each page as a _____ or at the bottom of each page as a _____.

9. Formatting can be saved as a style and used in future documents.

   Many word processing programs have _____ that use predefined styles.

   Templates also include text that is always used, such as a title and headings.

   Many word processing programs have an AutoFormat feature that formats documents as they are typed. AutoFormat automatically creates symbols (such as   when :) is typed), fractions (such as ½ when 1/2 is typed), and ordinal numbers (such as 1st when 1st is typed).

   Exploring Online
   Understanding word processing means learning many unique terms, such as fonts, styles, headers, and points. PC Webopaedia — an online encyclopedia that maintains a comprehensive word processing glossary — can help you become familiar with these new terms. After you have learned the basics, the WordInfo Web site will help you create attractive, well-written documents. To learn more about word processing resources on the Web, visit the Exploring Computers Web page (www.scsite.com/expl.htm) and click Word Processing.

D. Saving a document

   Three common ways to save a document are to:_____ , _____ , or _____.

E. Printing a document

   1. _____ shows how a document will look when printed.

   2. _____ orientation prints so the document is taller rather than wider.

      _____ orientation prints so the document is wider rather than taller.

      To print a document, click File on the menu bar and then click Print to display the Print dialog box.

Evaluating the Results

True/False

Instructions: Circle **T** if the statement is true or **F** if the statement is false.

T F 1. Word processing software is the least used productivity software, because the typewriter is used for virtually all personal and business communications.

T F 2. Word processing software allows words, sentences, or entire sections to be added, deleted, or rearranged without having to retype an entire document.

T F 3. As text is typed, the **ENTER** key must be pressed at the end of each line so that the text will continue on the next line.

T F 4. Copying duplicates a selected section of text on the Clipboard.

T F 5. Margins usually are measured in points.

Matching

Instructions: Write the letter of a description from the column on the right in front of each term in the column on the left.

_____ 1. Creating

_____ 2. Editing

_____ 3. Formatting

_____ 4. Printing

_____ 5. Saving

a. generating one or more paper copies of a document

b. making changes to a document

c. storing a copy of a document to prevent work from being lost

d. authorizing the production of a document

e. making a document by entering text with the keyboard

f. changing the appearance of a document

g. distributing a document among coworkers and soliciting opinions

Multiple Choice

Instructions: Circle the correct response.

1. Which of the following is not a type of document produced with word processing software?
   a. reports
   b. newsletters
   c. spreadsheets
   d. Web pages

2. Which key moves the insertion point to the beginning of a line?
   a. **HOME**
   b. **LEFT ARROW**
   c. **END**
   d. **RIGHT ARROW**

3. What editing feature is used to search for synonyms for words in a document?
   a. spell checker
   b. thesaurus
   c. grammar checker
   d. search and replace

4. Font size is measured in what unit?
   a. points
   b. inches
   c. centimeters
   d. rods

5. Landscape orientation is used to print what type of documents?
   a. personal letters
   b. long reports
   c. interoffice memos
   d. tables with many columns

Fill in the Blanks

Instructions: Place the correct word(s) in the blank in each sentence.

1. _____ is the process of moving through a document to view its various parts.

2. The _____ of a word processor automatically moves existing text to the right as new text is typed.

3. Most word processors have a(n) _____ menu that can be used to cut or copy selected text and then paste it in another location.

4. When the alignment of text is _____ , words are spread out in each line so that the right and left margins are even across the document.

5. The _____ feature shows how a document will look when it is printed.

Examining the Issues

1. Although many homes and almost all businesses in America use word processing software, people in Europe have been slower to embrace this popular productivity software. In France, applications for schools and jobs usually still are written by hand and often with a fountain pen. Handwriting is thought to show greater formality and more personality, while documents produced with word processors are seen as impersonal. Handwriting analysis even plays a role in hiring decisions. Will word processing ever become as widely accepted in Europe as it is in America? Are documents produced with word processors more impersonal than those written by hand? Why? For what kind of documents, if any, do you feel word processors are inappropriate?

2. Templates are somewhat controversial word processing tools. Templates provide the formatting, and often some of the text, for standard documents. They are available for letters, resumes, memoranda, reports, brochures, pleadings, theses, and other documents. Advocates claim that templates free people to concentrate on the content, instead of the format, of a document. Critics argue that memorable work requires an understanding of the work in its entirety, including how its parts are put together. Templates, they maintain, result in bland, uninspired, look-alike drivel. For what type of
documents are templates appropriate? For what type of work are they unsuitable? Why? With the availability of templates, is it still necessary to learn conventional formats for letters, resumes, reports, and theses? Why or why not?

Investigating the World

1. Most word processing software offers similar features, but all word processing software is not the same. Menus, toolbars, layouts, fonts, and other features differ from one application to the next. Visit a software vendor and compare at least two types of word processing software (such as Word and WordPerfect). How are they similar? How are they different? Which one is easier to use? Why? Is either application compatible with (able to work with) any other applications? If so, which one(s)? What is the price of each application? Based on what you have learned and how you anticipate you would use a word processor, which software would you be more likely to purchase? Why?

2. In addition to complete word processing programs such as Word and WordPerfect, word processing software also is built into integrated packages such as Microsoft Works and ClarisWorks, and even included with some operating systems (for example, a word processing program called WordPad is included with Windows). Visit a software vendor and try a word processing program that is part of an integrated package or included with an operating system. With which application or operating system is the program associated? Which features described in this lab are included in the program? What features are not included? Is the program easy to use? Why or why not? What are the advantages and limitations of the software? Would you be happy with a word processing program that is included with an integrated package or an operating system, or would you prefer a complete word processing program? Why?

Working with Spreadsheets

Summarizing the Lab

6

Instructions: Use the *Working with Spreadsheets* interactive lab to complete the following outline.

I. What is a spreadsheet and spreadsheet software?

A _____ is a worksheet that resembles a table for organizing numbers.

Manual spreadsheets have been used for a long time to manage and keep track of data. Spreadsheet software can perform these same operations and many more in a spreadsheet file that may contain as many as 255 spreadsheets.

The first electronic spreadsheet, VisiCalc, was introduced in 1979.

II. Spreadsheet files

Electronic spreadsheets have the distinguishing features shown in Figure 6 on the next page.

The cell address for the cell at the intersection of column D and row 5 is _____.

A spreadsheet has more than 16,000,000 cells. When a cell is selected (clicked), a heavy border surrounds the cell and the cell reference displays in a Name box above and to the left of the worksheet window. Data entered in the cell appears to the right of the Name box in what is called the _____.

A range is a series of adjacent cells. A range is selected by dragging. Ranges are designated with the beginning cell reference, a punctuation mark (such as a colon), and then the ending cell reference (for example, C5:F5 is the range of cells in row 5 from column C to column F).

Exploring Online

The Web is a great resource for information on spreadsheets. The Spreadsheet Tools and Standards page, for example, provides recommendations on basic spreadsheet design, while The Spreadsheet Page includes tips, templates, and links to online tutorials for Microsoft Excel, Lotus 1-2-3, and Corel Quattro Pro. The Web sites of Microsoft, Lotus, and Corel also provide extensive information on their specific spreadsheet software. For more information on working with spreadsheets, visit the Exploring Computers Web page (www.scsite.com/expl.htm) and click Spreadsheets.

III. Cells

Three types of data or information can be input into a cell:

- _____

- _____

- _____

Inputting text, then numbers, and finally formulas is a useful order for entering data.

A. _____ usually are the first thing added to a spreadsheet.

Labels help identify the data and organize the spreadsheet. Labels should be descriptive to make data input easier.

In most spreadsheet programs, cells are eight to ten characters wide. If text is longer than the width of the cell, the text flows into the adjacent cell on the right when the adjacent cell is empty. Cell width can be adjusted using a feature known as AutoFit or by dragging the column boundary to the right or left.

The _____ key completes an entry. Depending on how the spreadsheet program is set up, when the ENTER key is pressed the cell may remain selected or the selection may move to an adjacent cell. With some spreadsheet programs, an entry also can be com-pleted by pressing the TAB key or an arrow key or by clicking the Enter box (check mark) in the formula bar.

B. After the text is entered, the next step is to input the _____ , or values.

Some spreadsheet programs allow a cell to be protected when it contains data that should not change. Protecting a cell prevents it from being altered accidentally. The cell's contents cannot be changed until the protection is removed.

C. Formulas perform calculations and display the resulting values.

_____ adds the values in selected cells and places the total in the last selected cell.

In most spreadsheet programs, formulas are preceded by a symbol, such as = or @, to distinguish them from text.

Formulas can be copied from one cell and pasted into another cell using the Copy and Paste buttons on the toolbar or the Copy and Paste commands on the Edit menu. When a cell is copied, its contents are placed in a temporary storage location called the Clipboard. A moving border, often called a marquee, surrounds the copied cell.

When a formula is pasted, the cell references are updated automatically (changed to fit the new location). This automatic updating is called _____.

Cell references can be kept constant (unchanged) by placing a dollar sign in front of the column letter and row number. When the cell reference, D5, appears in a formula, the cell reference is not updated. The value in cell D5 is used whenever the formula is calculated, even if the formula is copied to a new location. This is called absolute referencing. When only the column is kept constant (as in $D5), only the row is kept constant (as in D$5), or neither the row nor the column is kept constant (as in D5), it is called relative referencing.

D. The _____ button is used to format a number as a percent.

Other toolbar buttons also can be used to format numbers. The Currency Style button formats numbers as dollar amounts. The Comma Style button formats numbers with commas between periods. The Increase Decimal and Decrease Decimal buttons increase or decrease the number of digits displayed after the decimal point.

Exploring Windows

Many spreadsheet applications are available in versions designed to take advantage of the features of Windows. Some of these spreadsheets include:

- Corel Quattro Pro
- Lotus 1-2-3
- Microsoft Excel

Files created in one of the spreadsheet applications listed above usually can be saved in a specific format so they can be read by one of the other spreadsheets.

IV. Changing data in a spreadsheet

With a manual spreadsheet, when one value changes, all related values must be recalculated manually. When data in an electronic spreadsheet is changed, formulas are recalculated automatically and new values are generated.

A. The capability to automatically recalculate is called

_____.

Because what-if analysis allows users to see the results of changing data in a spreadsheet, it is a powerful decision-making tool.

Another decision-making tool provided by most spreadsheet software is called goal seeking. Goal seeking determines the input value necessary for a formula to achieve a desired result or goal.

B. Many spreadsheet programs come with built-in formulas called

_____.

Some spreadsheet programs have more than 200 built-in functions. These functions are separated into several categories such as:

- _____   • _____   • _____

- _____   • _____   • _____

- _____   • _____   • _____

C. _____ gives a description of circumstances when and how a function would be used.

D. Using a _____, you can transfer current data from the World Wide Web directly into your spreadsheet.

Exploring Your Computer

Create one of these simple manual spreadsheets on paper:

- A school budget spreadsheet, with rows for expenses such as tuition, books, lab fees, club dues, and supplies. Provide data for two different quarters or semesters and add up the total expenses.

- A win-loss record spreadsheet, with rows for team names and columns for wins, losses, and ties. Find the total wins, losses, and ties for the league, as well as the total number of games played.

If you have access to a spreadsheet program, such as Excel, Quattro Pro, or Lotus 1-2-3, create an electronic version of your spreadsheet, entering data in at least four different rows or columns.

V. Graphs and charts

In addition to making numerical calculations very quickly, the results can be turned into charts and graphs that graphically show relationships.

Charts and graphs put numerical relationships in a more concrete form so they can be recognized more quickly and be understood easily.

The charts and graphs available with spreadsheet applications are called _____ because they are used in making business decisions.

There are several different types of graphs. When selecting a graph type, it is important to choose the one that best portrays the data. The three most common graph types are:

- Line charts — to represent a trend over time

- Bar charts — to show relationships among data

- Pie charts —to illustrate relationships of parts to a whole

Other graph types include scatter charts, area charts, doughnut charts, and radar charts.

Evaluating the **Results**

True/False

Instructions: Circle **T** if the statement is true or **F** if the statement is false.

T F 1. A spreadsheet file can contain as many as 255 spreadsheets.

T F 2. Each spreadsheet has 65,356 columns and 256 rows.

T F 3. Text or labels usually are the last thing added to a spreadsheet.

T F 4. Labels should be descriptive to make it easier to input data.

T F 5. When data is changed in a spreadsheet, formulas are recalculated automatically and new values are generated.

Matching

Instructions: Write the letter of a description from the column on the right in front of each term in the column on the left.

_____ 1. Tab sheets

_____ 2. Columns and rows

_____ 3. Cells

_____ 4. Charts and tables

_____ 5. Functions

a. organize data vertically and horizontally

b. feature that automatically adjusts column width

c. illustrate relationships among data

d. where columns and rows meet

e. typically at the bottom of a window

f. below and to the right of a spreadsheet window

g. built-in formulas

Multiple Choice

Instructions: Circle the correct response.

1. Which of the following can be used to view different parts of a spreadsheet?
   a. scroll bars
   b. scroll arrows
   c. scroll boxes
   d. all of the above

2. Where is cell D5 located?
   a. on tab sheet D in row 5
   b. at the intersection of column D and row 5
   c. on tab sheet D in column 5
   d. at the intersection of column 5 and row D

3. Which key should be pressed after inputting each number in a spreadsheet?
   a. **ENTER**
   b. **SPACEBAR**
   c. **END**
   d. **ISERT**

4. What is the capability to automatically recalculate formulas when values are changed?
   a. relative referencing
   b. AutoFit
   c. what-if analysis
   d. cell addressing

5. What are analytical graphics?
   a. charts and graphs used in making business decisions
   b. text used to identify data
   c. built-in formulas that are broken up into several categories
   d. multiple series of adjacent cells

Fill in the Blanks

Instructions: Place the correct word(s) in the blank in each sentence.

1. A(n) _____ is a worksheet that resembles a table for organizing numbers.

2. Data entered into a cell displays to the right of the Name box in what is called the _____.

3. _____ adds the values in selected cells and places the total in the last selected cell.

4. The updating of cell references when a formula is pasted into another cell is called _____.

5. Some spreadsheet applications have a program called _____ that describes how to use many of the features available.

Examining the Issues

1. Designing a successful spreadsheet can be a daunting task. Good spreadsheets not only produce correct results, they also help users understand those results. The following guidelines have been offered for designing effective spreadsheets:

    - Use specific titles and documentation

    - Date spreadsheets internally

    - List any assumptions made

    - List or print formulas

    - Check input values with an IF function

    - Check computations with values that have known results

    Why is each guideline important? What other practices can help make spreadsheets more effective? How?

2. Many business decisions involve risk. In a process called risk analysis, managers use spreadsheets to weigh the degree of risk. Various outcomes (returns) are suggested, a probability is assigned to each outcome, expected values are computed, and then the expected values are totaled. For example, a manager considering investing in FlimFlams or JibJabs may perform the following risk analysis:

Possible Return	Probability (FlimFlams)	Probability (JibJabs)	Expected Value (FlimFlams)	Expected Value (JibJabs)
$50,000	30%	50%	50,000 x .30 =15,000	50,000 x .50 =25,000
$10,000	60%	20%	10,000 x .60 = 6,000	10,000 x .20 = 2,000
$0	10%	30%	0 x .10 = 0	0 x .30 = 0
	Total Expected Values		$21,000	$27,000

Based on this risk analysis, in which product would a manager invest? Why? What other factors may influence a manager's decision? What risks are involved in risk analysis?

Investigating the World

1. Recent surveys show that word processing software and spreadsheet applications are the most used productivity applications. In addition to recording income and expenses, spreadsheet programs have assumed a wide range of other functions. A medical center that treats accident victims also supplies spreadsheets estimating the types, frequency, and costs of treatments for insurance purposes. A noted restaurant uses spreadsheet software to inventory its wine cellar, determining the popularity of each vintage and reducing what once was a two-day chore to a one-hour task. Visit a local business and interview someone familiar with how the company uses spreadsheet software. What application is used? Why? For what purposes are spread-sheets used? How has the use of spreadsheets benefited the company? What problems are associated with using spreadsheets?

2. In 1983, an innovative program developed by Mitch Kapor revealed the far-reaching capabilities of spreadsheet software. Kapor, a teacher of transcendental meditation, called his program Lotus 1-2-3 because it combined three elements (spreadsheets, graphics, and databases) in a spreadsheet program that was "as easy as one, two, three" to use. Lotus 1-2-3 dominated the spreadsheet market until 1991 when Microsoft released Excel 2, which was designed to take advantage of the Windows environment. Excel surged to the front of the market with features such as 3-dimensional graphics, auxiliary functions, wizards to guide users through complex tasks, powerful what-if tools, and easy-to-use database capabilities. Today, other spreadsheet programs, such as Corel Quattro Pro, have joined Lotus 1-2-3 and Excel. Visit a software vendor and compare two or more spreadsheet applications. How are they similar? How are they different? What is the cost of each? With what other applications are they compatible? Based on your comparison, which software would you recommend? Why?

Understanding the
Motherboard

Summarizing the Lab

7

Instructions: Use the Understanding the Motherboard interactive lab to complete the following outline.

I. What is a motherboard?

Computer program instructions are executed and data is manipulated in the system unit. A motherboard, sometimes called the main board or system board, is a _____ that contains most of the electronic components of the system unit.

II. Components of a motherboard

The components on a PC's motherboard are illustrated in Figure 7.

Figure 7

A. The _____ contains the control unit and the arithmetic/logic unit.

- The control unit can be thought of as the brain of the computer. It operates by repeatedly fetching program instructions from memory, decoding program instructions into commands the computer can process, executing the computer commands, and then storing the results of the instructions in memory. This process is called the machine cycle.

- The arithmetic/logic unit (ALU) contains the electronic circuitry necessary to perform arithmetic and logical operations on data. Arithmetic operations include addition, subtraction, multiplication, and division. Logical operations consist of comparing one data item to another. Based on the result of the comparison, different types of processing may occur.

B. The _____ chip contains a set of instructions called BIOS (Basic Input/Output System) that provides the interface between the operating system and hardware devices.

The _____ enables the ROM chip to maintain the date and time when the computer is turned off.

Many of the special-purpose computers used in automobiles, appliances, and so on, use small amounts of ROM to store repeatedly executed instructions.

C. _____ is the name given to the chips that are used for memory.

Memory stores three items:

- _____

- _____

- _____

Data and programs are transferred into and out of RAM, and data stored in RAM is manipulated by computer program instructions.

D. _____ are where additional add-on peripheral devices are attached to the motherboard.

E. The _____ connect hard disks to the motherboard.

Floppy disk drives and CD-ROM drives also may be connected to the motherboard. Each connector is designed so it can fit in only one type of socket and in only one correct position.

F. I/O connectors are used to join cables to input or output devices.

- The _____ connect the keyboard and the mouse to the motherboard.

- A _____ transmits data one bit at a time.

A bit (short for binary digit) can represent one of two values: on or off. Cables connecting serial ports generate little electrical interference and can be up to 1,000 feet long. Devices such as modems usually are connected to a serial port.

- A _____ transmits data eight bits, called a byte, at a time.

    A byte can represent 256 different data possibilities. Although faster than a serial port, electrical signals in a parallel cable tend to interfere with one another over long distances, so parallel cables usually are limited to 50 feet. Printers or tape backup devices usually are connected to a parallel port.

- The _____ transmits data one bit at a time, up to 20 to 40 times faster than a standard serial port and 3 to 5 times faster than a parallel port.

USB devices are connected to each other outside the system unit and then a single cable attaches to the USB port. Pointing devices, scanners, digital cameras, and speakers can connect to a USB port.

G. The _____ is where the switches and indicator lights plug into the motherboard.

- The _____ turns the computer on or off.

- The _____ reboots the computer.

- The _____ puts the computer into a power-saving mode.

H. The _____ is where the power supply plugs into the motherboard.

The power supply connector converts a wall outlet's AC (alternating current) power into DC (direct current) power, which is the type of power required by a computer.

Exploring Online

Intel Corporation is the primary manufacturer of processors for personal computers. Intel's Web site has information on processors Intel currently produces and future products that are under development. Other processor manufacturers, such as AMD, Cyrix, and IDT, also have information on the Web. To learn more about the latest processors and other components of the motherboard, visit the Exploring Computers Web page (www.scsite.com/expl.htm) and click Motherboard.

I. The _____ is the circuitry that connects all of the motherboard components together so they can communicate.

III. CPU choices

A. Processor speed is measured in _____ , which means millions of cycles per second.

Speed is determined by the system clock, which generates electronic pulses at a fixed rate and is used by the control unit to synchronize all computer operations.

B. Different processor types have different internal architectures:

- The _____ processor was designed to perform one operation at a time.

- The _____ processor added support for multimedia functions.

- The _____ was designed to perform more than one operation at a time.

- The _____ added video, audio, and 3-D enhancements.

- The _____ processor design was optimized for server performance.

    _____ , _____ , and _____ also make CPUs for PCs running Windows software.

The Motorola processor, which is found in Apple Macintosh and Power Macintosh systems, is an alternative to the Intel-style microprocessor.

> Exploring Windows
>
> Different users require different processing capabilities. For optimal performance, experts recommend that home users working with Windows have a 400 MHz or higher Pentium® II or III or 400 MHz Celeron™ processor, 32 megabytes of RAM (random access memory), and a SVGA (super video graphics array) standard resolution graphics card.

IV. ROM

A. _____ chips store information or instructions that do not change. ROM is described as _____ because it retains its contents even when the power is turned off.

Data or programs stored in ROM can be read and used but cannot be altered, hence the name *read only memory*.

B.   The _____ is the program stored in ROM that starts, or boots, the system when it is first turned on, or reboots it later if the computer must be restarted.

The first part of the boot process is the _____ , which verifies that the computer hardware is connected properly and operating correctly.

The second part of the boot process is loading the _____ . The operating system coordinates activities of hardware devices and allows users to run application software.

BIOS also stores information about the system's hardware setup (configuration) and can provide the first line of security for a system.

V.   RAM

A.   _____ is the name given to chips that store programs and data that can change. RAM is described as _____ because the programs and data in RAM are erased when the power to the computer is turned off.

The size of memory (RAM) is measured in kilobytes (K or KB) — approximately 1,000 bytes, or megabytes (MB) — approximately one million bytes.

B.   PCs use memory packages called _____ or _____ They consist of several RAM chips mounted on a small circuit board.

SIMM packages are available in capacities from _____ .

DIMM packages are available in capacities from _____ .

RAM speed, which is printed on the top of each chip, is measured in _____ (billionths of a second). Lower numbers mean higher speeds.

_____ is the primary type of memory chip packaged on SIMMs and DIMMs.

VI.   The system and expansion buses

Buses connect components on the motherboard and provide for communication with the CPU.

- The _____ directly connects the CPU to memory.

- The _____ provides a communications channel between the CPU and devices attached to the computer.

A.   The system bus consists of two components:

- The _____ connects the CPU and RAM.

- The _____ connects the CPU with cache memory.

Cache memory is fast memory that the CPU uses to store frequently accessed information.

B. The expansion bus carries signals from expansion slots to the system bus. Add-on devices connect to expansion slots.

Three types of expansion slots typically are found on modern computers:

- _____ slots, found in almost all systems, have a narrow and slow bus so less information can travel along it.

- _____ slots, the most common slot type in today's PCs, have a bus with a direct line to the CPU for rapid data transport.

- _____ slots, used only for video cards, have a bus that connects the video card directly to the CPU and system RAM.

Exploring Your Computer

What type of processor is in your computer? How much random access memory (RAM) does your computer have? Are any peripheral devices, such as a sound card or modem, attached to your computer through the motherboard's expansion slots?

Evaluating the Results

True/False

Instructions: Circle **T** if the statement is true or **F** if the statement is false.

T F 1. The two components of the CPU work together using the program stored in memory (RAM) to perform the processing operations.

T F 2. A processor running at 450 MHz can complete up to 450 million machine cycles every second.

T F 3. The speed of each new processor type always is slower than its predecessor.

T F 4. ROM is described as volatile because the programs and data in ROM are erased when the power to the computer is turned off.

T F 5. SIMMs have 168 pins along one edge of the circuit board, and DIMMs have 72 pins.

Matching

Instructions: Write the letter of a description from the column on the right in front of each term in the column on the left.

_____ 1. Pentium®

_____ 2. Pentium® with MMX™

_____ 3. Pentium® II

_____ 4. Pentium® III

_____ 5. Pentium® III Xeon™

a. design optimized for server performance; runs at speeds of 500 MHz and higher

b. designed to work in dual-processor systems; runs at speeds of 233 – 450 MHz

c. design added new support for multi-media functions; runs at speeds of 166 – 233 MHz

d. designed for the original IBM personal computer; runs at a speed of about 4.77 MHz

e. designed with video and audio enhancements and a CPU serial number; runs at speeds of 450 – 500 MHz

f. designed to perform one operation at a time; runs at speeds of 60 – 200 MHz

g. designed for PCs costing less than $1,000 and features optimized core instructions; runs at speeds of 500 – 600 MHz

Multiple Choice

Instructions: Circle the correct response.

1. What is *not* stored in memory (RAM)?
   a. the program that starts, or boots, the system when you first turn it on
   b. the application program that tells the computer what to do
   c. the data being manipulated
   d. the operating system that directs and coordinates the computer

2. Why might a computer user want to access the BIOS Setup program?
   a. to check the date and time settings for year 2000 compliance
   b. to update disk drive settings because a new drive has been added
   c. to cure a system instability problem by changing a memory management setting
   d. all of the above

3. What is the primary type of memory chip packaged on SIMMs and DIMMs?
   a. DRAM (dynamic RAM)
   b. SDRAM (synchronous dynamic RAM)
   c. DROM (dynamic ROM)
   d. SDROM (synchronous dynamic ROM)

4. How many devices can use the internal bus at one time?
   a. only one
   b. only two
   c. only three
   d. only four

5. Which of the following is not a type of expansion slot typically found on modern computers?
   a. ISA (Industry Standard Architecture) slots
   b. PCI (Peripheral Component Interconnect) slots
   c. MIS (Multimedia Ingredient Support) slots
   d. AGP (Accelerated Graphics Port) slots

Fill in the Blanks

Instructions: Place the correct word(s) in the blank in each sentence.

1. The _____ , which contains most of the electronic components of the system unit, sits in the main housing along with the power supply.

2. The _____ consists of the control unit and the arithmetic/ logic unit.

3. _____ are where additional add-on devices, such as video display cards and sound cards, attach to the motherboard.

4. The _____ is a collection of parallel wires embedded in the motherboard that allows communications among the CPU, RAM, hard disk controller, I/O controller, and PCI/AGP controller chips.

5. _____ is fast memory the processor uses to store information it is processing.

Examining the Issues

1. Consider the differences between ROM and RAM. In terms of your own memory, what kind of information do you have in your ROM memory? What kind of information do you have in your RAM memory? Why do you think special-purpose computers, such as those used in automobiles or appliances, use ROM instead of RAM?

2. ENIAC, the first computer, filled an entire room, yet it was less powerful than today's laptop computers. During the 1980s, the power of PCs expanded tenfold, and over the past twenty years the capacity of RAM has more than doubled every two years. As the processing power and memory of personal computers grow, it is becoming increasingly difficult to define personal computer and to separate it from its larger cousins. How do you define personal computer? Do you think your definition will still be valid twenty years from now? Why or why not?

Investigating the World

1. If you own or have access to a personal computer, unplug it and take the cover off the system unit. Make a sketch of the motherboard and try to identify as many components as you can. Be careful not to touch any of the components. Referring to the computer's User Guide, list the specifications for some of the components described in this lab (for example, the CPU, CPU speed, bus speed, RAM type, RAM capacity, expansion slots, and so on).

2. Visit a computer vendor and compare one of its less expensive personal computer systems to one of its more expensive computer systems. Make a table that shows the differences between motherboard components (type of CPU, RAM capacity, and so on). Do you think the differences justify the discrepancy in price? Why or why not? Are there any other factors (such as included software) that may also affect the price disparity?

Scanning Documents

Summarizing the Lab

8

Instructions: Use the Scanning Documents interactive lab to complete the following outline.

I. What is a scanner?

A scanner is an input device that takes information on paper and converts it into _____ that can be used by a computer.

Most computers are digital and process data (text, sound, graphics, or video) that has been converted into a numeric (digital) value. The binary number system, which uses only the digits 0 and 1, is used to represent all values.

Inputting data with a scanner is a form of source data collection (or source data automation) because a scanner eliminates the manual entry of data. Source data collection can save time, minimize inputting errors, and help automate other parts of the processing cycle.

II. Types of scanning

The two types of scanning are _____ and _____ .

A. _____ creates a graphical representation of the page being scanned, electronically capturing the entire page of text or artwork.

The digital information collected by the scanner can be stored on disk, processed by a computer, and then printed or displayed separately or merged into another document such as a newsletter. This procedure, called image processing, has become widely used. As a result, image scanners play an increasingly important role in many offices.

Scanning
Documents

Exploring Online

The World Wide Web allows people to display graphics files. Many companies scan pictures of their products to display on the Internet. For example, the scanned-in cover for *Exploring Computers: A Record of Discovery, Third Edition* displays on the Exploring Computers Web site.

Some companies scan pictures or documents for clients and deliver them through the World Wide Web. One such company is Root Technologies. For more examples of and information about scanning, visit the Exploring Computers Web page (www.scsite.com/expl.htm) and click Scanning.

B. _____ attempts to find patterns in the scanned image and translate them into meaningful information.

Two common scanning processes that accomplish this are optical character recognition and bar code scanning.

1. _____ results in data that can be processed by word processing software.

OCR is a specialized area — scanners that can read one type of symbol may not be able to read another. OCR devices range from hand-held wands to large machines that automatically read thousands of documents per minute. The standard OCR typeface, called OCR-A, can be read easily by both machines and people. OCR-B is a set of characters widely used in Europe and Japan. OCR technology is improving to include a wider assortment of characters, symbols, and even handwriting. OCR is used frequently for turn-around documents, such as billing statements, which are designed to be returned to the organization that created them.

_____ is used with image scanners to convert text images into data that can be used by word processing software. An entire page of text is scanned, and then the software attempts to identify individual words and letters.

OCR software usually is able to identify more than 98 percent of the scanned material. Any unidentified text is displayed for the operator to correct.

2. _____ are designed to process bar codes, one type of optical code. A _____ consists of a set of vertical lines, each of which represents either 1 or 0, and spaces. Every pattern of 1s, 0s, and spaces is associated with a specific _____ that identifies a product by name.

The UPC bar code, used for grocery and retail items, can be translated into a ten-digit number. This number is printed at the bottom of the bar code and can be input manually if the bar code reader fails. Bar codes also are used by the postal service, shipping services, railroads, and book publishers. Hand-held guns, hand-held wands, or stationary readers can read bar codes.

Two other forms of scanning plus recognition are optical mark recognition (OMR) and magnetic ink character recognition (MICR). Optical mark recognition identifies the position of a mark and often is used to process standardized questionnaires or test answer sheets. Magnetic ink character recognition (MICR) is used by the banking industry to interpret characters that have been printed on the bottom of a check with a special magnetized ink. These characters indicate the bank, account number, check number, and the amount of the check after it has been cashed.

III. The image scanning process

Image scanning without OCR results only in a collection of _____ that can be used by a software application.

Pixels, or picture elements, are the individual dots that can be illuminated to form an image on the computer screen.

Image scanning takes place using one of the four types of scanners shown in Figure 8.

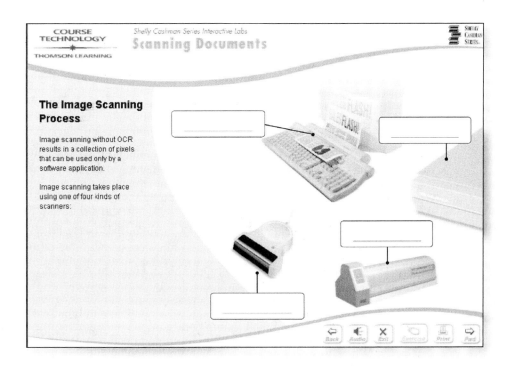

Figure 8

A. A _____ works much like a copy machine.

1. A light source within the scanner illuminates the image located against the scanner's glass surface.

2. A _____ moves along the page picking up reflected light and projecting it to pivoting mirrors, which then project it to a lens.

3. The lens focuses the light onto a _____ , which converts it into electrical current of different voltages that correspond to the brightness of the reflected light.

4. The current is sent to an _____ , which changes the voltages into digital impulses.

5. The _____ are sent to the computer to be used by different software applications.

Hand-held scanners are adequate for scanning small areas; however, because they depend on a steady hand, the overall quality can deteriorate when scanning large images.

> **Exploring Your Computer**
> Scanners usually are connected to computers through a SCSI (small computer standard interface). Other types of SCSI devices include CD-ROM drives and tape backup systems. Do you have a scanner, or any other type of SCSI device, attached to your computer?

B. Scanned images may be _____ , _____ , or _____ . The scanning process is slightly different for each.

1. When scanning in _____ , the analog-to-digital converter stores the voltage readings as either black (1) or white (0).

2. Scanning images in _____ means that the voltage readings are stored as shades of gray, instead of only black and white.

    Images scanned in grayscale are like black and white photographs.

3. To scan images in _____ , the scan head makes three passes under the image. Each pass uses a different color filter (red, green, or blue) to modify the color of the light. The full-color image is made by combining the results of the three passes.

The cost of scanners, both hand-held and full-page, has decreased significantly during the past few years. Full-page color scanners are the most expensive. Color images require more storage space than black and white images of the same resolution.

C. The term _____ refers to the number of pixels per square inch displayed on the screen.

The resolution, or clarity, of the image depends on the number of pixels and the distance between them. The greater the number of pixels and the closer they are, the better the resolution. Resolution is defined in _____ , or dpi.

1. The _____ the resolution at which an image is scanned, the lower the quality of the final image.

   Because they must be moved over an image by hand, the resolution of hand-held scanners is lower than the resolution of flatbed scanners.

   Low resolution images generally take up _____ memory.

2. The _____ the resolution at which an image is scanned, the higher the quality of the final image.

   High resolution images can take up _____ of memory.

   High quality laser scanners are used by newspapers, publishers, and service bureaus because of their accuracy.

Exploring Windows

Windows supports Plug-and-Play hardware devices. When a Plug-and-Play scanner is attached to a Windows computer, Windows automatically detects the scanner and installs the appropriate software, or drivers, to control it.

Evaluating the Results

True/False

Instructions: Circle **T** if the statement is true or **F** if the statement is false.

T F 1. Two common scanning processes that convert scanned input into more meaningful information are optical character recognition (OCR) and bar code scanning.

T F 2. The most commonly used scanner, the sheet-fed scanner, operates much like a copy machine.

T F 3. When the light source within a flatbed scanner illuminates the image, white portions of the page reflect less light than images or words.

T F 4. To create a full-color image, the scan head in a flatbed scanner makes three passes under the image.

T F 5. A low resolution image generally takes up a great deal of memory.

Matching

Instructions: Write the letter of a description from the column on the right in front of each term in the column on the left.

____ 1. Scanning

____ 2. Image scanning

____ 3. Scanning plus recognition

____ 4. Bar code scanning

____ 5. Black and white scanning

a. takes information on paper and converts it into digital form

b. employs an analog-to-digital converter that stores voltage readings as either 1 or 0

c. Identifies the position of a mark made on a standardized form

d. creates a graphical representation of the image scanned and electronically captures an entire page

e. processes a type of optical code consisting of vertical lines and spaces

f. attempts to find patterns in a scanned image and translate them into meaningful information

g. combines three different scan passes to create an image

Multiple Choice

Instructions: Circle the correct response.

1. What are the two types of scanning?
   a. optical character recognition (OCR) and bar code scanning
   b. black and white scanning and color scanning
   c. image scanning and scanning plus recognition
   d. hand-held scanning and sheet-fed scanning

2. What is used with image scanners to convert text images into data that can be processed by word processing software?
   a. OCR software
   b. RBG software
   c. UPC software
   d. OMR software

3. Which of the following is not a scanner used for image scanning?
   a. sheet-fed scanner
   b. bar code scanner
   c. hand-held scanner
   d. flatbed scanner

4. In a flatbed scanner, what converts light focused by the lens into electrical current containing different voltages?
   a. a scan head
   b. a pivoting mirror
   c. an analog-digital converter
   d. a light-sensitive diode

5. When capturing an image in color, which of the following is not one of the color filters used to modify the color of light directed at the image?
   a. red
   b. yellow
   c. blue
   d. green

Fill in the Blanks

Instructions: Place the correct word(s) in the blank in each sentence.

1. _____ results in data that can be processed by word processing software.

2. A(n) _____ consists of a set of vertical lines and spaces.

3. Each pattern of 1s and 0s processed by a bar code scanner in a store is associated with an _____ that identifies the product by name.

4. Some scanners scan images in _____ , which means the voltage readings are stored as shades of gray, instead of only black or white.

5. The term _____ refers to the number of pixels per square inch displayed on the screen.

Examining the Issues

1. Using an image scanner and a computer, a photograph can be altered subtly to create a desired effect. The cover of a news magazine once showed a photograph of a famous person who had been accused of a grisly crime. The photograph had been retouched to give the figure a more sinister appearance. Some people objected to the cover, claiming that it implied the defendant was guilty even before he had been tried. Others insisted, however, that the photograph was not offered as an exact representation but as a graphic portrayal of the seriousness of the accusation. Under what circumstances, if any, is it appropriate to enhance a photograph using a computer? What can be done to prevent retouched photographs from being accepted as literal truth?

2. To produce accurate information, a computer requires accurate input. Inaccurate information caused by inaccurate data can be worse than no information at all. The need for accurate input is summarized by the computer jargon term GIGO, which stands for Garbage In, Garbage Out. Of the three input devices described in these labs (the mouse, the keyboard, and scanners), which is most likely to result in accurate input? Why? Which is least likely to result in accurate input? Why? What factors have the greatest influence on input accuracy?

Investigating the World

1. The cost of scanners has decreased significantly during the past few years. Visit a computer vendor and examine the scanners available. What type of scanner (drum, hand-held, sheet-fed, or flatbed; black-and-white, grayscale, or color) is least expensive? Why? What type of scanner is most expensive? Why? For what purposes would the most inexpensive scanner be adequate? When would the most expensive scanner be required? If you were purchasing a scanner for yourself, which type would you buy? Why?

2. Bar code scanners are used by retail stores, supermarkets, and libraries. Visit an organization that uses bar code scanners and interview a manager to find out how the scanners are used. What kind of information is the organiza-tion able to collect? How is the information used? In what ways does the information obtained through the use of scanners benefit the organization or the organization's clientele? Was the organization able to keep track of the same information before it used scanners? Why or why not?

Setting Up to Print
Summarizing the Lab
9

Instructions: Use the Setting Up to Print interactive lab to complete the following outline.

I. Printing: the computer revolution

Low-cost, high-quality printers help computer users create professional quality documents.

Output that is printed is called hard copy. Printing requirements differ greatly, and as a result, printers have been developed with varying speeds, capabilities, and printing methods.

_____ and _____ components work together to change electronic documents into a printed page.

II. Printer choices

Printers fall into the two categories illustrated in Figure 9 on the next page.

A. _____ printers are inexpensive and can print on continuous forms, but they can be noisy.

Front striking impact printers strike the mechanism that forms the character against an inked ribbon, which in turn strikes the front of the paper (similar to a typewriter). Hammer striking impact printers strike a hammer against the back of the paper, pushing the paper against an inked ribbon and the desired character. Most impact printers use continuous-form paper composed of sheets connected together for a continuous flow through the printer.

_____ printers are an example of an impact printer.

Dot matrix printers produce images by striking wire pins against an inked ribbon. The combination of small dots forms a character, much like the characters produced by combinations of light bulbs on an electronic scoreboard. Draft-quality printing uses the minimum

COURSE
TECHNOLOGY

THOMSON LEARNING

Shelly Cashman Series Interactive Labs
Setting Up to Print

SHELLY
CASHMAN
SERIES.

Printer Choices

Figure 9

number of dots to form a character. Letter quality (LQ) and near letter quality (NLQ) printing, in which a higher-quality look is achieved by overlapping dots, is done at slower speeds. Most dot matrix printers have moveable print heads and are designed to print in a bidirectional manner (that is, from left to right and then back again from right to left). The speed of impact printers with moveable print heads is measured in characters per second or cps.

Band and chain printers, which print using a rotating band or chain, are impact printers used for high-volume output on large computer systems. These printers print an entire line at a time.

B. _____ printers output at a much higher resolution than impact printers and are nearly silent.

Nonimpact printers use chemicals, laser light, or heat to transfer an image to paper. The resolution of most nonimpact printers is from 300 to 720 dpi (dots per inch). The resolution of a dot matrix printer is typically less than 100 dpi. The speed of nonimpact printers is measured in pages per minute or ppm. The majority of nonimpact printers use individual sheets of paper stored in a removable tray that slides into the printer case.

The most common types of nonimpact printers are the _____ printer and the _____ printer.

Ink jet printers spray tiny drops of ink onto the paper to form a character or image. Because the print nozzle can contain from 50 to more than 100 small holes, they produce high-quality print or graphics. Ink jet printers are quiet and print at rates of 1 to 8 ppm. Ink jet printers require good quality, single-sheet paper to prevent the ink from bleeding.

A third type of nonimpact printer, called a thermal printer or thermal transfer printer, uses heat to transfer colored inks from ink sheets onto the printing surface.

> Exploring Online
>
> Major suppliers of computer printers include Hewlett-Packard, Epson, and Canon. To learn more about these companies and the different types of printers they offer, visit the Exploring Computers Web page (www.scsite.com /expl.htm) and click Printers.

C. How a laser printer works

1. A laser beam converts data from the computer into _____ .

2. A _____ reflects the light against the surface of a photosensitive drum.

3. Areas of the drum touched by the reflected laser beam pick up an _____ which attracts _____ that collect on the drum.

4. As a sheet of paper is fed past the rotating drum, the drum transfers the toner pattern to the paper using _____ and _____ .

Laser printers used with personal computers range in speed from 4 to over 30 pages per minute (ppm). Laser printers usually come with a large number of built-in fonts, or character sets. Laser printers used with individual personal computers start at less than $300. They represent the fastest growing segment of the printer market.

III. Connecting the printer

The printer is connected to the computer using a _____ , which contains eight lines for data along with other lines for grounding and synchronization.

The electrical signals in a parallel cable tend to interfere with one another over a long distance, so parallel cables usually are limited to 50 feet. Personal computer parallel cables are usually six to ten feet long.

Most PCs communicate to the printer using a _____ , which is referenced as _____ . This port can send eight bits, or a single byte, to the printer at one time.

Parallel ports are used most often to connect devices that send or receive large amounts of data.

> Exploring Your Computer
>
> Is there a printer attached to your computer? Is it attached directly to the computer through a parallel port or is it connected via a network? Is your printer an impact or nonimpact printer? What brand of printer is it?

IV. Setting up a printer

Attaching a printer to a computer system involves configuring the computer so that it knows the capabilities of the printer and is able to communicate with it.

A. A _____ is a program that converts the computer's printing instructions into commands the printer can understand.

In order for a printer to function, an appropriate printer driver must be installed on the computer. Most printer manufacturers include driver software with their printers; many operating systems also include printer drivers.

B. Communicating with the printer

The computer can communicate with the printer in two ways:

1. High-resolution page information can be fed line by line to a variety of printers without internal processing capabilities using the printer's _____ .

2. A _____ enables the computer to describe elements of the page individually to printers that have internal processing capabilities, such as laser printers.

Using a page description language allows a document created on one computer to be printed on another computer with a different printer, as long as the second printer has a compatible page description language.

V. Preparing documents

A. Print setup features, which control the way documents are printed, are set using the _____ dialog box. This dialog box presents basic options, such as the pages and number of copies to print.

B. The _____ dialog box presents more options, such as paper size, layout, and orientation.

Portrait orientation means the paper is taller than it is wide. This is the orientation used for most correspondence. Landscape orientation means the paper is wider than it is tall. This orientation often is used for tables with a large number of columns.

C. The _____ tab in the Properties dialog box can be used to add special effects, such as reversing or mirroring the image.

VI. Printing text

_____ are files that are used by a computer's operating system to display text in different styles.

Fonts are a combination of typeface (character sets such as Times Roman, with a specific appearance and shape) and point size (the height of the type; each point is approximately 1/72 of an inch). Often, two different files exist for each font: a bitmap version and an outline version. TrueType fonts require only a single file.

A. _____ , also called screen fonts, are pixel-based fonts designed to display on the screen the way the printed page will look.

In bitmap fonts, each pixel (which equals a bit) is illuminated individually by a combination of graphics hardware and software.

B. _____ , which describe, or trace, the typeface using curves and angles, are used for printing. This enables the printer to print the font in any size.

C. _____ fonts are a kind of outline font that is designed also to be used on the screen.

TrueType fonts appear in the printed document the same as they appear on the screen, which is important in applications such as desktop publishing. In Windows applications, the names of TrueType fonts are preceded by TT. TrueType fonts are included withWindows.

VII. Using fonts

A. When text is emphasized by making it italic or bold, it is called changing the _____ of the text.

A style is a customized format applied to characters. Underlining is another style.

B. When the computer sends an outline font that is not in the printer along with the document, it is called _____ the font.

The downloaded font is stored in the printer's memory while the document is printing.

Because most printers are 1,000 times slower than computers, they have a buffer that temporarily stores information, allowing the computer to dump output into the buffer and continue processing.

Exploring Windows

Windows allows users to drag and drop graphical representations of files to perform certain functions. For example, a word processing document can be printed by dragging the icon representing the document to a printer icon and then dropping it.

VIII. Printing grayscale images

Black-and-white printers reproduce grayscale images using a _____ _____ , which appear as shades of gray when viewed at a distance.

A. _____ , a technique generally used by impact printers, is creating a shade of gray by printing dots of the same size and varying their number.

B. _____ , which can be done using nonimpact printers to give a more realistic effect, is creating a shade of gray by printing a regular pattern of dots and varying their size. Newspapers often use this technique to reproduce photographs.

IX. Printing color images

Color documents are printed by making multiple passes over the paper using _____ , which are mixed on the page to produce the desired hue.

Color output is more attractive, but it is slower and more expensive for all printer types.

Evaluating the Results

True/False

Instructions: Circle **T** if the statement is true or **F** if the statement is false.

T F 1. Impact printers produce output with much higher resolution than nonimpact printers and are nearly silent.

T F 2. The printer is connected to the computer using a parallel cable, which contains eight lines for data along with other lines for grounding and synchronization.

T F 3. Most PCs communicate with the printer using the serial port.

T F 4. Often, two different files exist for each font: a bitmap or pixel-based version and an outline version that describes the characters using curves and angles.

T F 5. Color documents are printed by making multiple passes over the paper using primary colors and mixing the colors on the page to produce the desired hue.

Matching

Instructions: Write the letter of a description from the column on the right in front of each term in the column on the left.

____ 1. Printer driver

____ 2. Low level printer command

____ 3. Page description language

____ 4. Dithering

____ 5. Halftoning

a. is used by newspapers to reproduce photographs and can be done with nonimpact printers

b. presents specialized print options, such as changing the intensity and detail of the image

c. feeds high resolution page information to a printer without internal processing capabilities

d. configures the computer so it knows the capabilities of the printer

e. is used by impact printers because they can print only dots of a single size

f. is capable of sending eight bits, or a single byte, to the printer at one time

g. enables a computer to specify elements of a page individually

Multiple Choice

Instructions: Circle the correct response.

1. Which of the following is a type of impact printer?
   a. dot matrix printer
   b. laser printer
   c. ink jet printer
   d. all of the above

2. In a laser printer, the laser beam converts data from the computer into what?
   a. grayscale images
   b. bitmap fonts
   c. pulses of light
   d. toner particles

3. How is the parallel port referenced in a PC system?
   a. LPT1
   b. MIDI
   c. COM1
   d. RJ-11

4. For Windows applications, what window is used to set basic options such as what printer to use, in what orientation to print, and the size and source of the paper?

   a. Page Description dialog box
   b. Print Setup dialog box
   c. Print dialog box
   d. Advanced Options dialog box

5. What kind of fonts, included with the Windows operating system, are designed to look the same when they are printed as they appear on the screen?

   a. bitmap fonts
   b. screen fonts
   c. TrueType fonts
   d. outline fonts

Fill in the Blanks

Instructions: Place the correct word(s) in the blank in each sentence.

1. _____ printers make images by striking a print head against the paper.

2. _____ printers transfer an image to the screen without striking it.

3. A(n) _____ is a program that converts the computer's printing instructions into commands the printer can understand.

4. _____ are files that are used by a computer's operating system to display text in different styles.

5. When the computer sends an outline font to the printer along with the document, it is called _____ the font.

Examining the Issues

1. An office secretary recently expressed anxiety about the future. Low-cost, high-quality printers, powerful personal computers, and easy-to-use software have had a substantial impact on the office environment. Company executives who once had secretaries prepare all their reports and correspondence now are creating, editing, and revising their own documents. Is there still a place for the secretary in the modern office? Are the secretary's fears justified? Why or why not? How will the computer revolution affect traditional jobs?

2. When computers first were used in business, many people envisioned the paperless office — a place where most documents would exist only electronically as a computer file. Yet surprisingly, many offices actually are using more paper now than in the past. Environmentally concerned organizations are uneasy about the waste of paper. Some companies reuse unwanted documents by printing on the reverse side for internal reports. Many offices recycle used paper. Even if all paper were recycled once, however, it would have little impact in light of the historical increases in paper usage. Quieting the conscience of the over-consumer may even result in an overall net increase in consumption and waste. How have computers and low-cost printers contributed to the waste of paper? What could be done to decrease the amount of paperwork?

Investigating the World

1. Several questions should be considered before you purchase a printer:

   - What type of output (text, graphics, professional correspondence, etc.) will you produce?

   - Who will use, or receive, the output?

   - How much output will you need to produce?

   - Are multiple copies required?

   - Is color essential?

   - Are different fonts necessary?

   - Where will the printer be used?

   - Is the sound or speed of the printer a factor?

   - Is cost an issue?

   Answer each of these questions according to your current needs. Then, visit a computer store and find at least two printers that fit your requirements. Write the name of each printer and note its advantages and disadvantages. If you were going to purchase one of these printers, which would you buy? Why?

2. People are becoming increasingly concerned with ecological and health issues related to computer printers. Toner cartridges and printer ribbons, which must be changed periodically, are taking up space in the world's landfills. It has been estimated that more than 12 million toner cartridges are disposed of each year. Workers in large offices complain about the noise pollution generated by several impact printers working at once and the possible effects on their hearing. Some office employees are anxious about the ozone emitted by poorly maintained laser printers. Ozone has been linked to
respiratory problems, nausea, headaches, and possibly cancer. Using a library or other research facility, prepare a report on the ecological and health problems associated with printers and the steps that are being taken to address these problems.

Configuring your
Display
Summarizing the Lab

10

Instructions: Use the *Configuring Your Display* interactive lab to complete the following outline.

I. How does the computer create a display?

A computer's display system consists of the components illustrated in Figure 10.

Figure 10

A monitor coupled with an input device, such as a keyboard, in a single unit is called a VDT (video display terminal). VDTs usually are connected to larger, multi-user computer systems.

II. The monitor

A computer's monitor is very similar to an ordinary _____ , but instead of tuning in broadcasts, it receives signals from the computer.

Personal computers typically use CRT, or cathode ray tube, technology. Technically, a CRT is the large tube inside a monitor. The front part of the tube is the display surface or screen.

Most portable computers use flat panel displays that employ either liquid crystal display (LCD) or gas plasma technologies. In an LCD display, a liquid crystal deposited between two sheets of polarizing metal is aligned by an electrical current. The liquid crystal prevents light from passing through and creates an image on the screen. This technology is used in digital watches, clocks, and calculators. Gas plasma screens substitute a neon gas for the liquid crystal material. Although gas plasma screens offer better resolution, they are more expensive and use more energy than LCD screens.

A. Computer monitors have _____ to adjust the picture.

B. The screen size of computer monitors is measured _____ , in inches, across the opposite corners of the screen.

The most widely used monitors are equivalent in size to a 17-inch television screen, but monitors designed for desktop publishing, graphics, or engineering applications come in larger sizes, such as 21 inches.

Exploring Online

Popular display manufacturers on the Web include Sony, NEC, ViewSonic, and MAG Innovision. In addition, Hercules Computer Technology hosts the World Wide Web Monitor Database, which includes a listing of monitor manufacturers and models with screen sizes. For more information on display technologies, visit the Exploring Computers Web page (www.scsite.com/expl.htm) and click Monitors.

C. The two main types of computer displays are
_____ and _____ .

  1. A _____ monitor displays shades of a single
color on black.

Monochrome monitors are less expensive than color monitors
and often are used by businesses for word processing, order
entry, and other applications that do not require color. Using
gray-scaling, which converts an image into pixels that are shades
of gray, some monochrome monitors can display good quality
graphic images.

  2. A _____ monitor displays images in full color.

Color monitors are widely used with all types of computers
because color monitor prices have fallen and most of today's
software is written to display information in color.

RGB monitors combine _____ ,
_____ , and _____ color beams
inside the video tube to reproduce the entire range of visible
colors.

In the simplest combinations, eight colors can be generated by
combining the RGB color beams: black (no color), red only, green
only, blue only, magenta (red and blue), yellow (red and green),
blue-green (blue and green), and white (red, green, and blue). As
the intensity of the beams varies, many more hues can be
generated.

D. A mask perforated with holes breaks the light beams into small dots
on the computer screen. The distance between the dots, or
_____ , determines how much detail the monitor
can display.

The perforated mask is called a shadow mask. The light beams move
across and down the screen. Interlaced monitors illuminate every
other line, then return to the top to illuminate the lines skipped.
Noninterlaced monitors illuminate the entire screen more quickly in
a single pass. The speed at which the entire screen is redrawn is
called the refresh rate. If the refresh rate is too slow, images on the
screen may oscillate or flicker.

III. What is a graphics display?

The computer's display is made up of tiny squares called picture
elements, or _____ .

The number of pixels actually displayed is determined by a combination
of the software in the computer, the capability of the video adapter
board, and the monitor itself.

A. The number of pixels on the screen determines the screen's
_____ . A display's resolution is measured in the
number of pixels _____ the screen times the
number of pixels _____ the screen. A typical
resolution for a computer display is 800 pixels across by 600 down.

Monitor resolution is important, particularly when the monitor is
used to display graphics or other nontext information. Due to
separate development, printer resolution is expressed in dots per
inch while monitor resolution is expressed in pixels per inch, which
is dependent on dot pitch.

B. The number of colors that can be displayed on the screen at one time
is called the _____ . The range of available colors
also is called the _____ .

   1. In an _____ graphics system, 256 colors can be
   displayed on the screen.

   2. In higher bit graphics displays, more bits are used to determine
   each pixel's color. Typical bit depths are _____ (65,536
   colors) and _____ (16.7 million colors). Twenty-four
   bit images also are called _____ images.

   Most PC color monitors display at least 256 colors at one time.

Monitors with _____ capability can self-adjust to
the display signals of many different computer systems.

Multisync, also called multiscanning, monitors are designed to work
within a range of frequencies.

Exploring Your Computer

How large is the monitor on which you are working (remember, monitor size is
measured diagonally across the screen)? How many colors does your monitor
display? What is your monitor's resolution? What brand is your monitor?

IV. What is a graphics card?

The _____ is an expansion card that is installed in one
of the slots of the PC. It converts pixel information into
_____ for display on the monitor. The card is
equipped with its own memory, called _____
(VRAM), to store the pixel information.

A. _____, are developed to define the resolution, number of colors, and other properties for graphic cards. The graphics card in widespread use today is Super Video Graphics Array (SVGA).

B. _____ allows a higher number of colors and degree of resolution. Typical SVGA resolutions are _____ and _____ with thousands or even millions of colors.

Other video graphics standards include: CGA, or color graphics adapter, (640 x 200 with four displayed colors — one of the first cards to display color images), Hercules (720 x 348 with no color), and EGA or enhanced graphics adapter (640 x 480 with sixteen displayed colors). A concept called backward compatiblity allows graphics cards capable of higher resolution to run programs requiring lower resolution.

C. When more colors are displayed or resolution is increased, more _____ is required to store the pixel information. The amount of memory on the graphics card determines the maximum combination of resolution and color depth.

D. Most modern computer systems use a high-speed bus dedicated to graphics, called a _____ . This bus bypasses the standard bus and communicates directly with the CPU, updating the screen at a much higher speed.

V. System configuration

Once a graphics card is installed, an application can be run from the _____ to configure the system based on the new hardware. You then can modify the display's resolution and color depth through the _____ settings in the Display Properties dialog box.

Exploring Windows

In addition to configuring the resolution and number of colors displayed by your monitor, you can use the Control Panel window to change your display's appearance and your monitor's energy saving features. Right-clicking the Windows desktop, clicking Properties, then clicking the Appearance, Background, or Screen Saver tabs in the Display Properties dialog box allows you to change these options.

Evaluating the Results

True/False

Instructions: Circle **T** if the statement is true or **F** if the statement is false.

T F 1. The computer's display system consists of a video display, monitor cable, graphics card, and display driver software.

T F 2. A display's resolution is measured by the number of pixels across the screen times the number of pixels down the screen.

T F 3. Screen images drawn from a smaller palette have more gradual tones.

T F 4. When more colors are displayed or resolution is increased, less memory is required to store the pixel information.

T F 5. Resolution can be increased by sacrificing color depth, and vice versa.

Matching

Instructions: Write the letter of a description from the column on the right in front of each term in the column on the left.

____ 1. Monichrome	a.	describes a monitor that displays images in shades of a single color on black
____ 2. RGB	b.	is a high-speed local bus dedicated to graphics
____ 3. Resolution	c.	is a mask perforated with holes that break up the light beams as they pass through
____ 4. Color depth	d.	is determined by the number of pixels on the screen
____ 5. Graphics card	e.	is a type of monitor that displays images in full color
	f.	converts pixel information into video signals for display on the monitor
	g.	is the number of colors that can be displayed on the screen at one time

Multiple Choice

Instructions: Circle the correct response.

1. What can be adjusted using the external controls on a computer monitor?
    a. resolution and color depth
    b. bus type and VRAM
    c. contrast and brightness
    d. all of the above

2. How is screen size measured?
    a. diagonally, in inches, across opposite corners of the screen
    b. down, in inches, from the top left corner to the bottom right corner
    c. across, in inches, from the top left corner to the top right corner
    d. as total screen area, in square inches

3. Which is not one of the three color beams used to reproduce the entire range of visible colors in a color monitor?
    a. red
    b. yellow
    c. blue
    d. green

4. What is dot pitch?
    a. the amount of memory on the graphics card
    b. the distance between pixels on the monitor screen
    c. the time required for the monitor to communicate with the CPU
    d. the number of bits used to determine each pixel's color

5. What level resolution is used by most monitors sold today?
    a. CGA
    b. EGA
    c. SVGA
    d. VGA

Fill in the Blanks

Instructions: Place the correct word(s) in the blank in each sentence.

1. Monitors with _____ capability can self-adjust to the display signals of many different computer systems.

2. The computer's display is made up of tiny squares called

    _____ .

3. _____ images are also called *true color* because their smooth range of color allows photorealistic images.

4. Some computer systems have a high-speed bus dedicated to graphics, called a(n) _____ , which bypasses the standard bus and communicates directly with the CPU.

5. You can change display resolution, color depth, and more through the _____ window.

Examining the Issues

1. The demand for larger computer displays continues to grow — even as the monitors themselves become thinner. Business users are seeing the benefits of larger screens which allow you to see more open windows at once and have a better view of documents and large spreadsheets. Users also are turning to thinner LCD monitors, which require only a quarter of the desk space of a comparable CRT and which do not create distortion. Lower heat emission, combined with power savings of up to 40 percent over comparable CRTs, appeal to just about everybody. At what point do you think the increase in display size and decrease in monitor width will stop? What will monitors be like ten years from now? Will employers use larger screens as a way to demand more productivity from workers?

2. Today, nearly all personal computers use a monitor. Although monitors are sometimes sold separately, it is hard to imagine buying a personal computer without one. Personal computers have even been sold with the monitor and system unit together in a single case, like the Apple Macintosh computer introduced in 1984. Will monitors still be the most popular computer display device twenty-five years from now? Why or why not? How might monitors be different?

Investigating the World

1. Visit a computer vendor and obtain information about the highest and lowest priced monitors. Record the names of the monitors, their costs, and the features available with each. Do you think the more expensive monitor is worth the difference in price? Why or why not? Examine a portable computer that uses a flat panel display. What type of screen is it (LCD or gas plasma)? How does the image compare with the most expensive CRT monitor? How does it compare with the least expensive CRT monitor?

2. Questions have been raised about health issues related to computer monitors. Although some believe that prolonged work at a monitor is less hazardous than a sunny day at the beach, others feel continued exposure to electromagnetic emissions from monitors can cause pregnancy problems or cancer. Certain European countries have published guidelines placing limits on monitor emissions. In America, many organizations have developed conservative policies, limiting the number of hours pregnant women work with a display screen or closely monitoring electromagnetic emissions. Using current periodicals or online services, research some of the health issues connected with computer monitors. Are the concerns justified? What is being done to address them? What steps, if any, should personal computer users take to protect themselves?

Maintaining your
Hard Drive

Summarizing the Lab

11

Instructions: Use the *Maintaining Your Hard Drive* interactive lab to complete the following outline.

I. What is a hard disk?

A hard disk is a hardware device that can store a large number of _____ in the form of files.

A hard disk is called storage because it stores programs and data when they are not being processed. memory, or RAM, on the other hand, temporarily holds programs and data when they are being processed. Memory is fast, short-term, and volatile. Storage is slower, long-term, and nonvolatile. Other forms of storage include floppy disks, optical discs (CD-ROMs), and magnetic tape.

> ### Exploring Windows
> Microsoft Windows includes various tools for maintaining a hard drive. Among these are ScanDisk, which checks for and fixes errors on the hard disk; DriveSpace, which compresses the hard disk to free more space; and Disk Defragmenter, which reorganizes the files stored on the hard disk so they can be accessed more efficiently.

II. How a hard disk works

Most hard disks contain between one and four _____ coated with an oxide material that are mounted on a rotating spindle.

Personal computer hard disk drives typically are identified with the letter C, while the letters A, B, and D identify floppy disk and CD-ROM drives. Hard disks often are fixed, or permanently installed, in the computer system (although some portable computers have removable hard disk drives called disk cartridges). Floppy disks are a portable storage medium. Hard disk platters usually are aluminum, but some newer disks use glass or ceramic materials. Floppy disks (also called diskettes or floppies) consist of a circular piece of flexible mylar plastic coated with an oxide material and housed in a protective jacket. Both hard disks and floppy disks are examples of magnetic storage media.

Each surface of a hard disk's platter can be used to store data. _____ heads attached to access arms swing out over the top and bottom surfaces of each platter.

The clearance between the heads and the disk surface is about ten millionths of an inch. If some form of contamination gets on the surface of the disk or if the read/write heads are jarred out of alignment, the heads can collide with and damage the disk surface and cause a loss of data. This event, known as a head crash, can be extremely costly in terms of both time and money.

A. _____ is the short delay that results when the read/write heads move to where the beginning of the data is located.

Magnetic disks are referred to as direct-access storage devices because the computer can go immediately to the location where the desired data is stored. Magnetic tape, on the other hand, is considered a sequential storage medium because the computer must read each record in order on the tape until it locates the desired record.

The access time for a disk drive consists of two factors: _____ and _____ .

1. _____ is the time it takes the read/write head to move across the width of the disk. Average seek time is considered the time it takes to move about halfway across the disk's width.

Seek time is the largest part of total access time.

2. _____ is the delay while the platter rotates so the first item of data moves under the heads. The time it takes for half a rotation to occur is considered the average rotational delay.

Access time for a hard disk is between ten and twenty milliseconds (thousandths of a second), while access time for a floppy disk varies from about 150 milliseconds to 300 milliseconds. Hard disk access time is significantly less for two reasons: (1) a hard disk spins ten to twenty times faster than a floppy disk; and (2) a hard disk is always spinning, but a floppy disk spins only when a read or write command is received.

B. The read/write heads read data from the disk by picking up _____ generated by the magnetic particles on the

coated platters. The signals are converted into _____
and loaded into the computer's main memory unit.

C. When writing data to the disk, data from the computer's memory
    unit is converted into _____ , which are stored as
    positive and negative _____ on the platter.

Exploring Online

A number of hard drive manufacturers exist on the Web, including Seagate
and Western Digital.

If a problem is experienced with the hard drive, the DriveSavers Data Recovery
home page gives advice and assistance in recovering lost data. To learn more
about maintaining your hard drive, visit the Exploring Computers Web page
(www.scsite.com/expl.htm) and click Hard Drive.

D. _____ is the time it takes to move
    a given amount of data to or from the disk. Data transfer rate is
    measured in _____ (million characters) of data
    transferred per second.

Some computers use a cache to improve the apparent speed at which
data is transferred to and from a disk. Cache is an area of memory set
aside for the data most often read from the disk. When data is
requested, the software looks first in the cache. If the data is there,
the slower disk read operation is avoided. A cache program is
included with the Windows operating system.

Access arms, with their attached read/write heads, move in fixed
patterns that cause the data to be written to both sides of the disk in
concentric circles called _____ . Each track is divided
further into a number of equal parts called _____ .

Tracks, cylinders, and sectors are defined on the disk surface when
the disk is formatted. The formatting process also erases any data
on the disk, analyzes the surface for defective spots, and establishes a
directory to record information about stored files. Hard disks and
floppy disks must be formatted before they can be used for
secondary storage.

Two methods can be used to write data to the disk:

1. In the _____ , the data is written to the disk
    track-by-track across a single surface, and then continued on the
    next surface.

Each sector contains a specified number of bytes; with PCs, for example, each sector holds 512 bytes. When data is requested from a disk using the sector method, the surface, track, and sector where the data is stored are indicated.

2. In the _____ , all tracks of the same number on each surface create a cylinder. Data is written to the same track on each of the surfaces before the read/write heads move on to the next track.

When data is accessed from a disk using the cylinder method, the cylinder, recording surface, and record number are specified.

III. How a hard disk stores files

Storage capacity is a function of the number of tracks per inch (tpi) and the number of bits that can be stored per inch of track (bpi).

Hard disk storage is measured in _____ , each of which is equal to over _____ typewritten pages of information. Typical computer systems have hard disks that can store up to _____ megabytes of data. Newer systems have hard disks that can store _____ .

Floppy disks store considerably less data than hard disks. High-density (HD) floppy disks can store 1.44 megabytes on a 3½-inch disk.

Data compression software, such as PKZIP and WinZip, can be used to store more data on a disk. Data compression reduces storage requirements by substituting codes for repeated patterns of data. The substituted codes are filed in a table, which is used to restore the compressed data to its original form.

When a file is stored on the hard disk, it is split into small, equal parts; each part is stored in one of the _____ on the hard disk. The space in which the file data is stored may not be _____ ; that is, it may not run across consecutive sectors.

IV. Fragmentation of the hard disk

If there are too few consecutive blank sectors to store a file, the hard disk skips to the next empty area and continues writing the file. When this happens repeatedly, the disk becomes _____ . This increases the time it takes the computer to read the file because each portion of the file must be accessed individually.

In sequential access storage devices, such as magnetic tape, fragmentation is not a problem because data is stored serially.

Exploring Your Computer

How much total storage space is on the hard drive in your computer? How much of the disk space is free and available? When was the last time your hard disk was defragmented? Has the hard disk been compressed by a disk compression program such as Stacker, Doublespace, or DriveSpace?

V. Maintaining an efficient hard disk

A. _____ is accomplished by reading each file into memory and then writing it to a contiguous area of the hard disk.

Operating systems such as DOS and Windows include a defragmentation utility.

B. _____ reduces the access time for the most frequently used files by moving them to the front of the hard disk.

The processes used to maintain the hard drive are illustrated in Figure 11.

C. Virus checking is a third procedure that should be performed regularly.

To prevent the loss of data, it also is important to back-up, or create another copy of, important programs and data on the hard disk. Floppy disks and magnetic tape commonly are used to back up at least some of the data stored on the hard disk of a personal computer.

Figure 11

Evaluating the Results

True/False

Instructions: Circle **T** if the statement is true or **F** if the statement is false.

T F 1. The access time for a disk drive consists of two factors: seek time and rotational delay.

T F 2. The time it takes for a full rotation of the hard disk to occur is considered the average rotational delay.

T F 3. Newer hard disks can sustain a transfer rate of one to two megabytes per second.

T F 4. The cylinder method of writing data to the disk increases the amount of movement, which decreases the speed.

T F 5. When a file is stored on the hard disk, the file is split into small equal parts, which are each stored in one of the sectors on the hard disk.

Matching

Instructions: Write the letter of a description from the column on the right in front of each term in the column on the left.

_____ 1. Platters

_____ 2. Access arms

_____ 3. Tracks

_____ 4. Sectors

_____ 5. Cylinders

a. narrow recording bands forming concentric circles around a hard disk surface

b. spindles on which disk surfaces rotate in the hard disk drive

c. rigid disks coated on either side with an oxide material that stores data as magnetic charges

d. mechanisms that swing out over the top and bottom surfaces of each hard disk

e. all concentric circles of the same number on each hard disk surface

f. two or more complete hard disk surfaces used to store the operating system

g. equal parts into which the concentric circles around a hard disk surface are divided

Multiple Choice

Instructions: Circle the correct response.

1. How many platters are mounted on a rotating spindle in most personal computer hard disk drives?
   a. one or two
   b. between one and four
   c. between eight and sixteen
   d. between fifty and one hundred

2. What is seek time?
   a. the time it takes to locate a file in memory and write it to the disk
   b. the time it takes for the platter to rotate so the first data item is under the read/write heads
   c. the time it takes to transfer data from the disk into memory
   d. the time it takes the read/write head to move across the width of the disk

3. In what method of writing data to the disk is data written track-by-track across a single surface, then continued down to the next surface?
   a. sector method   c. cluster method
   b. cylinder method   d. file method

4. Hard disk storage is measured in what units?
   a. kilobytes and centibytes   c. millibytes and kilobytes
   b. megabytes and gigabytes   d. dekabytes and megabytes

5. What procedure reduces access time for the most frequently used files by moving them to the front of the hard disk?
   a. defragmentation   c. optimization
   b. polarization   d. segmentation

Fill in the Blanks

Instructions: Place the correct word(s) in the blank in each sentence.

1. A(n) _____ is a hardware device that can store a large number of programs and data in the form of files.

2. _____ attached to access arms swing out over the top and bottom surfaces of each hard disk platter, generating electronic impulses.

3. The short delay that results as the read/write heads move to the beginning of where the data is located on a hard disk is known as

   _____ .

4. The time it takes to move a given amount of data to or from the disk is known as _____ .

5. A(n) _____ disk increases the time the computer takes to read files because each portion of the file must be accessed separately from noncontiguous sectors.

Examining the Issues

1. When a file is deleted from a hard disk, it is not physically erased or removed from the disk. Instead, the computer's operating system simply makes the sectors where the file was contained available for new data. Until another file is written to these sectors, the deleted file remains stored on the disk. What are the advantages of this system? What are the disadvantages?

2. It is estimated that data loss costs American companies approximately $4 billion each year. Data stored on hard disks can disappear as a result of natural disasters, computer viruses, or head crashes. Despite the risk, a study has shown that less than 35 percent of all companies have backup policies stipulating regular procedures for making copies of stored information. Why do so few companies back up their data? If you were the CEO of a large company, what backup policy would you establish? What would you do to see that it was enforced?

Investigating the World

1. Many companies store large amounts of information on hard disks that are permanently mounted inside the computer. As a result, the problem of data security has become an important issue. No company can afford to have sensitive information on customers or product development stolen by industrial spies or dissatisfied employees. Visit a large firm and interview an employee on data security. How are records protected? Who has access to sensitive data? Have there ever been problems with data security? If so, what measures have been taken to make sure the problems do not recur?

2. Visit a computer store and obtain information on the different types of hard disk drives available for personal computers. Summarize your findings and include data on price, storage capacity, and access speed. Calculate the cost per megabyte of storage for each disk drive. If you were purchasing a hard disk drive for your own personal computer, which would be best for your current needs? Why? Do you think the same disk drive would be adequate five years from now? Why or why not?

Evaluating Operating Systems
Summarizing the Lab

12

Instructions: Use the Evaluating Operating Systems interactive lab to complete the following outline.

I. What is an operating system?

_____ is a special collection of software that controls the operation of the computer hardware. The _____ (OS) is the primary component of the system software.

The role of the operating system is illustrated in Figure 12.

Figure 12

System software frees application software from having to handle tasks that are common among almost all programs that process data. Functions performed by system software include: starting up the computer; loading, executing, and storing application programs; storing and retrieving files; formatting disks; and sorting data files. The three major categories of system software are operating systems, utilities (programs that perform specific tasks related to managing computer resources or files), and language translators (programs used to convert programming instructions into machine language the computer can understand).

II. Parts of an operating system

An operating system consists of several parts: _____ , _____ , and _____ .

A. The _____ contains the most essential and frequently used commands in the operating system, which are called internal commands. When the computer is started, the kernel is _____ , or loaded, from the computer's hard disk into memory.

The kernel also is called the resident portion of the operating system. When the computer is turned on, the BIOS (Basic Input/Output System), a set of instructions stored in a read only memory (ROM) chip, performs a series of tests. The BIOS then searches for the operating system, starting with drive A and then going to drive C (usually the hard drive). When it locates the operating system, it loads the kernel into memory. In the Windows operating system, the kernel loads the registry (which contains system configuration information) and displays the desktop.

B. _____ are less frequently used commands that remain on the disk and are loaded into memory only as needed.

External commands are called the nonresident portion of the operating system. In DOS, these commands include format disk (FORMAT.COM), copy disk (DISKCOPY.COM), and check disk (CHKDSK.COM) as well as many others.

C. A _____ is the part of an operating system that enables the user to access the computer's features.

1. Using a _____ consists of typing instructions for the computer to execute. A _____ interface primarily employs a command language.

_____ is an example of a command-line interface.

A few experienced computer operators still feel a command-line interface is the fastest, most efficient way to perform certain tasks. Because of the large number of application programs written to work with MS-DOS, it was the operating system on many PCs in the United States. Many applications that work with MS-DOS actually use a menu-driven interface that allows users to select commands from on-screen lists.

2. With a _____ interface, the user interacts with the computer using a pointing device via graphical representations of the computer's resources.

_____ is an example of a graphical interface.

Graphical interfaces are intuitive (easy to use), consistent (the same for different applications), and user-friendly (simple to learn and forgiving of mistakes). To work efficiently, however, they require faster processors, greater disk space, and more memory than command-line interfaces. Improved hardware has addressed many of these difficulties, and the popularity of graphical interfaces continues to grow.

Prior versions of Windows (Windows 3.1 and earlier) were not actually operating systems but operating environments used with DOS that put a graphical interface on a command-line operating system.

> **Exploring Your Computer**
>
> Is your computer running Windows 3.1 or a later version of the Windows operating system? If it is Windows 3.1, the DOS operating system is running under the Windows 3.1 graphical user interface. Later versions of Windows are true operating systems, and DOS no longer is required.

III. Functions of operating systems

The operating system enables users and applications to interact with the _____ .

The main functions of an operating system are _____ , _____ , and _____ .

A. While using an application program, the operating system manages the use of _____ and monitors system performance.

System resource management — allocating or assigning the resources of the computer system — is the primary function of the operating system.

1. In a system where more than one program can run at one time, the operating system manages the sharing of the _____ time among the various programs. Each

program gets a _____ , which is a portion of CPU time.

A time slice usually is measured in milliseconds (thousandths of a second). Unless the system has a heavy work load, users may not even be aware when one program is set aside. The number of time slices given can be adjusted automatically or based on user-specified criteria.

2. The operating system assigns _____ (which may contain data being read or written, instructions to be executed, or data waiting to be processed) in several ways to maximize its use.

The operating system transfers the contents of _____ , areas of memory that contain data read from or written to an I/O device, to applications that request it. The operating system also assigns memory to _____ , reallocating unused memory and tracking how much is available.

Operating systems allocate at least some portion of memory into fixed areas called partitions, to which programs and data are assigned. Memory management programs in the OS can alter the size of partitions to accommodate programs and data.

Virtual memory management increases the effective, or virtual, limits of memory by expanding the amount of memory to include disk space. The OS transfers sections of data and program instructions, called pages, to and from memory and disk as required.

3. The operating system manages the flow of data to and from _____ and controls which applications may access which devices.

Because input and output devices use different commands and control codes to transmit and receive data, the operating system uses programs called device drivers to control these devices. Device drivers usually are supplied with the OS or by the device manufacturers.

B. Many applications split their work into separate tasks, or _____ , each of which uses a different resource, thus increasing performance. When one thread needs to communicate with another, it signals the _____ , which in turn notifies the other thread. The operating system also may support passing _____ between programs.

C. When an application needs to open a _____ for reading or writing, it requests access through the operating system. The operating system also may keep files secure by preventing unauthorized programs or users from accessing them.

Functions related to file and disk management include formatting hard disks and floppy disks, deleting files, copying files, and renaming files.

To insure file security, most multiuser operating systems employ a logon code that designates the application being used, a user ID that names the user, and a password that authenticates, through its confidentiality, the user's identity. All three items must be entered correctly before files can be accessed.

IV. Types of operating systems

Different kinds of operating systems have been designed to match the features and complexity of different computer architectures.

A. _____ operating systems handle only one person using one program at a time.

_____ is an example of a single program operating system.

Single-tasking operating systems were the first type of OS developed. Microsoft Corporation developed both PC-DOS (Personal Computer Disk Operating System) for IBM personal computers and MS-DOS (Microsoft Disk Operating System) for IBM-compatible PCs in 1981.

B. _____ enhance single program operating systems by automatically swapping programs in and out of memory to allow smooth transitions between them.

_____ and the _____ operating environment are popular examples of task switchers.

A shell program acts as an interface between the user and the operating system, offering a limited number of utility functions.

C. _____ operating systems enable several programs to run simultaneously, with varying degrees of effectiveness.

Exploring Windows

The Windows operating system was the much-anticipated successor to Microsoft's Windows 3.1 operating environment. Some of the advantages Windows offers over Windows 3.1 are pre-emptive multitasking that takes advantage of 32-bit microprocessors, Plug-and-Play for adding hardware devices, and a new *desktop* graphical user interface.

Although the CPU is capable of working on only one program instruction at a time, its ability to switch back and forth between programs makes it appear that all programs are running at the same time.

1. In a _____ multitasking system, processor access is controlled by the programs being used.

   _____ is a cooperative multitasking system.

   The Macintosh operating system was the first commercially successful graphical user interface when it was released in 1984. It has set the standard for ease of use and has been the model for most other graphical interfaces.

2. In a _____ multitasking system, the operating system has complete control over which program uses the processor and for how long.

   Highly interactive programs are considered _____ jobs and get more processor time. Low-priority tasks are _____ jobs and get less processor time.

   _____ and _____ are examples of pre-emptive multitasking systems.

   UNIX, developed by AT&T, is considered the most portable OS because it can be used with many different types of computers. Unlike Windows 3.1, Windows is a true operating system that does not require DOS. Windows can run programs written for DOS and earlier versions of Windows.

Although multitasking operating systems on PCs usually support a single user running multiple programs, some multitasking operating systems, called timesharing or multiuser operating systems, can support more than one user running more than one program.

Exploring Online

A host of Web pages discuss, illustrate, and promote various computer operating systems. Yahoo!, for example, lists the URLs of operating system Web sites dedicated to MS-DOS, Windows, Windows NT, OS/2, Mac OS, UNIX, and more. For more information on the features of different operating systems, visit the Exploring Computers Web page (www.scsite.com/exl.htm) and click Operating Systems.

D. In computers with more than one processor (called multiprocessing systems), a _____ operating system coordinates the processors, and maximizes their performance.

_____ and _____ are examples of multiprocessing systems.

Multiprocessing is implemented in two ways. In asymmetric multiprocessing, application tasks are assigned to a specific processor, each of which has its own amount of memory. In symmetric multiprocessing, application tasks may be assigned to whatever processor is available, and memory is shared among the processors.

E. A _____ operating system uses the computer hardware to simulate several virtual computers, each of which can run a different operating system. This allows software written for many different operating systems to be run on one computer.

With a virtual machine operating system, different operating systems can be run at the same time, and an appropriate OS can be assigned to each task. System resources are allocated to each operating system. VM is IBM's virtual machine operating system.

Evaluating the Results

Evaluating the Results

True/False

Instructions: Circle **T** if the statement is true or **F** if the statement is false.

T F 1. The entire operating system usually is stored in the computer's memory.

T F 2. Data read from or written to an I/O device, such as a disk drive, is stored in areas of memory called threads.

T F 3. When an application program needs to open a file on disk for reading or writing, it requests access through the operating system.

T F 4. In a pre-emptive multitasking system, low priority tasks, such as feeding characters to a printer, are given more CPU time and are considered foreground jobs.

T F 5. High-end workstations and mainframes are examples of single program operating systems.

Matching

Instructions: Write the letter of a description from the column on the right in front of each term in the column on the left.

____ 1. Single-tasking operating systems

____ 2. Task switching operating systems

____ 3. Multitasking operating systems

____ 4. Multiprocessing operating systems

____ 5. Virtual machine operating systems

a. automatically swap programs in and out of memory to allow smooth transitions

b. coordinate the CPUs in compouters that have more than one CPU

c. convert the instructions written by programmers into instructions a computer can understand

d. can handle only one person using one program at a time

e. use the computer hardware to simulate several computers that can each run a different OS

f. consist of programs that tell a computer how to produce information

g. enable several programs to run simultaneously with varying degrees of effectiveness

Multiple Choice

Instructions: Circle the correct response.

1. What part of the operating system is booted, or loaded into memory when the computer is started?
   a. utility programs
   b. the supervisor or kernel
   c. external commands
   d. the user interface

2. Which of the following is not a function of operating systems?
   a. application program development
   b. system resource management
   c. inter-process communication
   d. file management and security

3. MS-DOS is an example of what type of operating system?
   a. single program
   b. multitasking
   c. multiprocessing
   d. virtual machine

4. What is an example of a cooperative multitasking operating system?
   a. Microsoft Windows
   b. UNIX
   c. Macintosh System 7
   d. IBM's OS/2

5. What is the advantage of a virtual machine operating system?
   a. a non-cooperative program cannot keep control of the system until it is finished
   b. many jobs may run in the background without any loss in reaction time
   c. if one CPU fails, work is shifted to the remaining processors
   d. software written for many different operating systems can be run on the same computer

Fill in the Blanks

Instructions: Place the correct word(s) in the blank in each sentence.

1. The primary component of system software is known as the
   _____ .

2. The nonresident portions of the operating system, called
   _____ , are used less frequently and remain on disk until they are needed.

3. Using a(n) _____ interface consists primarily of typing instructions for the computer to execute, such as listing the files on a disk.

4. In a system where more than one program may run at one time, the operating system gives each program a(n) _____ , which is a portion of CPU time.

5. In a(n) _____ multitasking system, the operating system has complete control over which program uses the CPU and for how long.

Examining the Issues

1. Operating systems can be proprietary (limited to a certain model of computer) or portable (capable of running on many manufacturers' computers). Imagine you are the CEO of Computers and Advanced Technology (CAT), a company that specializes in laptop computers (company slogan: Life is better with a CAT on your lap). Your research department has developed an operating system that promises to make most other operating systems seem antiquated. Although designed to work specifically with CAT laptop computers, your programmers assure you the new operating system can be adapted to work with other computers. As CEO, you now have a decision to make. Should the new operating system remain proprietary, so that it only can be used with CAT computers, or should it be made portable, thus making it available to a wider spectrum of users? Explain your decision.

2. Manufacturers often release new versions of operating systems as they continue to make improvements. These versions sometimes are indicated by numbers following the operating system's name, such as MS-DOS 6.2, with whole numbers marking a major release and decimal numbers denoting minor updates. New releases are generally downwardly compatible, mean-ing that applications designed to work with earlier versions of the operating system will also work with the later version. For example, a word processing program designed to work with MS-DOS 3.3 probably will work with MS-DOS 6.2. Why are operating systems usually downwardly compatible? What are the advantages of downward compatibility?

Investigating the World

1. Find out which operating system is used on your or a friend's personal computer. Refer to the documentation that accompanied the operating system to determine what company manufactures the operating system, the operating system's version and release number, and the year it was produced. If possible, find out when the first version of the operating system was introduced, when the next version is expected, and how much is charged for upgrades. Describe the operating system. What kind of interface does it use? How does it perform system resource management, inter-process communication, and file management and security? What type of operating system is it? In general, what do you like about the operating system? What do you dislike?

2. Most application software (such as word processing, desktop publishing, spreadsheet, database, presentation graphics, communications, electronic mail, personal information management, project management, or games) are written for a specific operating system. Visit a store that sells computer software and make a list of at least five applications you would like to have on your personal computer. Find out the name of the operating system with which each of the applications you selected is designed to work. If an application does not work with the same operating system as the others, try to locate a similar one that does. Your goal is to find five applications that work with the same operating system. List the final five you choose and note the operating system they all use. What features, if any, did you have to give up to find five applications that use the same operating system?

Working at Your Computer

Summarizing the Lab 13

Instructions: Use the *Working at Your Computer* interactive lab to complete the following outline.

I. Working at the computer

As people spend more time working at computers, _____ while working is becoming increasingly important.

Incorrect posture can lead to _____ and _____ , that can cause permanent physical damage.

Good posture at the computer depends on two things:

- _____

- _____

A key characteristic of a well-designed workplace is flexibility. The workplace should be able to accommodate different sizes and tastes, to custom fit each worker.

II. What is ergonomics?

Ergonomics is an _____ that studies people's physical and cognitive characteristics in order to effectively design and arrange the things people use. Ergonomics can be used to design a _____ that properly positions a person's body in relation to the computer.

Ergonomics sometimes is called human engineering. About three decades ago, automobile manufacturers discovered they could boost sales by using ergonomics to design cars that were comfortable for drivers and passengers. In a similar way, an ergonomically designed workplace can raise productivity by minimizing fatigue and increasing worker satisfaction.

Exploring Online

Agile Corporation's Ergonomics Home Page and Intergraph Corporation's Ergonomics Office Guide are devoted to computer ergonomics.

Yahoo! also lists a variety of online companies that provide ergonomic accessories to make working at your computer safer and more comfortable. To learn more ways to improve working at your computer, visit the Exploring Computers Web page (www.scsite.com/expl.htm) and click Ergonomics.

III. Good posture

The goal of good posture is _____ and
_____ .

Good posture is achieved when the weight of the body is supported by the _____ , and the _____ provide lateral support.

Back, neck, or shoulder pain, the leading causes of lost work time, can all result from poor posture.

A. Ideally, sit with the _____ upright but not tense. The contour of the _____ should follow the slight natural curve of the lower back.

Slumping or leaning forward causes _____ .

If it frequently is necessary to use a telephone and computer at the same time, a telephone headset should be considered. Cradling a phone between the shoulder and neck can cause muscle strain.

B. The _____ should be right above the shoulders so that the spine can support its weight. The monitor should be placed so the top of the screen is at _____ .

The angle from the eyes down to the center of the screen should be about 20°.

Leaning the head back to look at the screen can _____ and cause _____ .

An adjustable monitor is recommended, and the screen should be tilted ±7° off perpendicular. The monitor should be about an arm's length away from the body. To minimize strain, a document holder that grips printed material next to the computer screen can be attached to the monitor or placed on your desk.

C. When working at the computer, both _____ should be back and relaxed. The distance between the _____ and the upper body should be small enough so that it is not necessary to lean forward.

Leaning forward or working with one shoulder pushed forward can lead to muscle strain in the _____ .

It is recommended that you stand up and walk around once each hour, and take at least a fifteen minute break every two hours.

D. The _____ should be parallel with the floor, allowing the wrist and hand to float over the keyboard. The angle between the forearm and upper arm will be _____ .

The most commonly reported problems associated with prolonged keyboard use are called repetitive stress injury (RSI) or cumulative trauma disorder (CTD). Government statistics indicate these injuries are responsible for half of all work-related illnesses.

1. Office desks often are too high for using a keyboard or mouse, forcing the forearm to be angled upward and wrist to arch, which strains the _____ .

   If the desk is too high, the keyboard can be lowered by attaching a _____ to the bottom of the desk, or the _____ can be raised to achieve the proper angle for the forearm.

2. Resting the _____ on a surface while typing causes _____ , or the upward tilting of the hand toward the arm, which is a major source of injuries.

   Ideally, the keyboard should be _____ on the desk, or even raised in front.

3. Your hands should be placed in a _____ position while typing. Pushing your hands to either side can _____ and cause injuries.

   Sufferers of carpal tunnel syndrome (CTS), a specific type of RSI, complain of weakness and pain in their wrists and hands and have difficulty grasping objects. CTS injuries are caused by pressure on the median nerve in the wrist, and can be permanently disabling.

Exploring Windows

The Microsoft Natural keyboard, designed specifically for Windows, is an ergonomically sound device that includes a built in wrist-rest below the keys themselves. The wrist-rest promotes good wrist positioning by raising the wrist to the same level as the hand and reducing dorsiflexion.

E. The angle between the spine and the thighs should be at least _____ . The thighs should slope _____ , and the feet should rest _____ , helping to keep the back in an upright position.

When sitting correctly, the weight of the body rests on the _____ . If the chair is too high, a _____ can be used to keep the body in the correct alignment.

Getting out and taking a walk at lunch can provide exercise and help to relieve stress.

IV. Protecting your eyes

Looking at the _____ can be stressful to the eyes. Two ergonomic factors can alleviate eyestrain: _____ and _____ .

A. The key to proper lighting is to make sure there is no _____ on the computer screen. Locating the screen _____ to light sources and away from overhead lights minimizes reflected light.

Glare can be reduced by: putting a _____ above the monitor, using an _____ , and keeping the _____ .

Ideally, the screen should be three to four times brighter than the room.

B. To minimize eyestrain, the distance from the eyes to the computer screen should be _____ .

The correct relationship between the body and the computer workstation is illustrated in Figure 13.

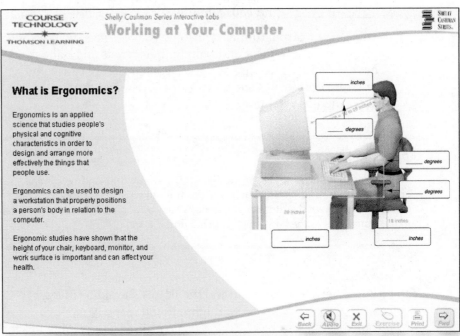

Figure 13

Workplace health considerations also should include the type and volume of work. People in stressful jobs need frequent breaks, and those who enter large amounts of data need regular breaks that incorporate hand and wrist exercises. Workers also can reduce tension and anxiety by eliminating or minimizing surrounding noise.

Computer users should be aware of the symptoms of repetitive stress injuries (soreness, pain, numbness, or weakness in the neck, shoulders, arms, wrists, or hands) and seek medical advice if these symptoms are experienced.

Exploring Your Computer

Take a minute to evaluate how you work at your computer. Are you seated comfortably, with good posture? Are your hands and arms in the proper position? Is your work area well lit? These are all important factors in creating a comfortable work environment and reducing the risk of computer-related injuries.

Working at Your Computer

Evaluating the Results

True/False

Instructions: Circle **T** if the statement is true or **F** if the statement is false.

T F 1. The goal of good posture is balance and ease of movement.

T F 2. Working with one shoulder pushed forward can reduce muscle strain in the shoulder and neck.

T F 3. Desks used in offices often are too high for using a keyboard or mouse, requiring the forearm to be angled upward and the wrist to arch.

T F 4. Raising the back edge of the keyboard reduces the problem of dorsiflexion, which is a major source of injuries.

T F 5. If you feel pressure on your tailbone when sitting at the computer, your chair is too high.

Matching

Instructions: Write the letter of a description from the column on the right in front of each term in the column on the left.

____ 1. 18 to 28 inches

____ 2. 20 degrees

____ 3. 28 inches

____ 4. 90 degrees

____ 5. 18 inches

a. the angle between the forearm and upper arm

b. the angle the screen is tilted off perpendicular

c. the angle from the eyes to the center of the screen

d. the distance from eyes to the screen

e. the distance from the floor to the desktop

f. the distance from elbow to the keyboard

g. the distance from the floor to the chair seat

Multiple Choice

Instructions: Circle the correct response.

1. On what does good posture at the computer depend?
   a. the user's awareness of the proper ways to hold the body while using the computer
   b. proper lighting in the room and a suitable distance from the computer screen to the user
   c. a computer workstation that allows the user to sit and hold the body properly while typing or using the mouse
   d. both a and c

2. How should the monitor be placed?
   a. so the top of the screen is 20° below eye level
   b. so the top of the screen is at eye level
   c. so the top of the screen is 20° above eye level
   d. so the bottom of the screen is at eye level

3. What should be the distance between the keyboard and the upper body?
   a. small enough so that your elbows are well behind your back
   b. small enough so that you do not have to lean forward to reach the keyboard
   c. large enough so that your wrists rest on the desk in front of the keyboard
   d. large enough so that you can fully extend your arms to reach the keyboard

4. Having your legs and feet in the right position will help to keep which of the following in the correct position?
   a. your back
   b. your wrists
   c. your head
   d. your hands

5. What is the key to proper lighting of the work environment?
   a. to make sure the room in which you work is brightly lit
   b. to make sure the computer screen is located close to overhead lights
   c. to make sure there is no glare on the computer screen
   d. to make sure light sources are parallel to the computer screen

Fill in the Blanks

Instructions: Place the correct word(s) in the blank in each sentence.

1. _____ can be used to design a workstation that properly positions a person's body in relation to the computer.

2. Good posture is achieved when the weight of the body is supported by the _____ .

3. When working at the computer, your _____ should be parallel with the floor, allowing the wrist and hand to float over the keyboard as you type.

4. Resting the wrists on a surface as you type causes _____ , or the upward tilting to the hand toward the arm, which is a major source of injuries.

5. A(n) _____ can help reduce reflected light on the computer screen, although it sometimes makes reading characters on the screen more difficult.

Examining the Issues

1. Once experienced mainly by line workers in poultry processing plants, repetitive stress injury (RSI) is a leading complaint today among computer workers. To date, offices have relied primarily on hardware answers to health concerns — suitable furniture and the proper placement of computer equipment. A product called Bodysavers, however, now offers a software solution. Bodysavers is a screen saver that, when there has been no input for a period of time, displays a message reminding computer users to exercise. Bodysavers also regularly interrupts users to show elementary hand and body stretches. Keeping in mind the cost of the software and the time users would spend not working, do you think Bodysavers would be a wise investment for a large office? Why or why not?

2. The introduction of computers in the workplace can cause not only physical problems, but emotional problems as well. A researcher from International Research Development, Inc. reported that about one-fourth of the work force may have experienced emotional stress related to the use of computers. Established workers described feelings of incompetence, loss of control, job insecurity, and anticipated demotion when computers were introduced in their offices. These feelings, which are sometimes called compuphobia, can have a tremendous impact on worker morale and productivity. Why are established workers more likely to experience compuphobia? If you were the manager of an office in which computers were being introduced, what might you do to prevent compuphobia?

Investigating World the

1. Imagine you are a consultant that specializes in workplace ergonomics. Using the information presented in this lab, prepare a checklist that can be used to evaluate a computer workstation. The checklist should contain a list of desirable characteristics and a scale with which each could be rated. Finally, decide on a passing grade for a workstation. After you have finished, visit the computer lab at your installation and use your checklist to evaluate one of the workstations. Did the workstation pass? If not, what has to be done for it to meet your approval? If the workstation was acceptable, how do you think it could be improved?

2. To minimize the risk of carpal tunnel syndrome, several ergonomically designed keyboards have been developed. Visit a computer vendor or use a computer equipment catalog to find at least two ergonomically designed keyboards. Who manufactures each keyboard? In what way are they different from standard keyboards? How do they reduce the chance of wrist injury? If possible, try out the keyboards. Compared to standard keyboards, are they more or less comfortable? Are they easier or more difficult to use? Why? How do the ergonomically designed keyboards compare to standard keyboards in terms of price? If they are more expensive, are they worth it? Why or why not?

Exploring the Computers of the **Future**

Summarizing the **Lab**

14

Instructions: Use the Exploring the Computers of the Future interactive lab to complete the following outline.

I. Computers of the future

Innovation in the computer industry has focused on developing computers that provide increased functionality and fit more naturally into people's lives and activities.

A. _____ and _____ are reducing the size of microprocessor chip components, leading to smaller computers with more processing capability and microcomputers embedded in objects and technological devices.

Early general-purpose computers such as the Mark I and ENIAC were room-sized, performed only a few calculations each second, and consumed so much electricity that when they were turned on city lights dimmed. The microprocessor chips in today's PCs are pocket-watch-sized, perform millions of instructions per second, and consume about as much electricity as a television set.

_____ are credit-card-sized pieces of plastic with embedded microprocessor chips that can store and process information and transactions.

The U.S. Marine Corps currently issues smart cards to recruits who use them instead of cash. Smart cards also can be used for employee time and attendance tracking and security applications. People may someday carry smart cards containing their complete medical histories, providing up-to-date medical records.

Exploring Online

Many exciting new developments in computing are taking place on the Internet. These online technologies, once thought to be far in the future, are being used today:

- Sun Microsystems's Java allows executable programs called *applets* to be run over the World Wide Web.
- Progressive Networks's RealAudio and RealVideo play live, real-time audio and video on the Web.
- Xing Technology's StreamWorks plays live video over the Internet.
- VRML, or Virtual Reality Modeling Language, enables designers to create 3-dimensional (3-D) Web sites.

To learn more details on these future technologies, visit the Exploring Computers Web page (www.scsite.com/expl.htm) and click Future.

B. _____ gives computers the capability to store and forward messages for their users, and to make voice annotations to documents.

Because people can speak much faster than they can type (about 200 words per minute compared to about 40 words per minute), some experts believe voice input eventually will be the most common way to operate a computer. Voice input is especially welcomed by people with certain disabilities.

C. _____ software enables a computer to recognize spoken commands by processing the physical sound waves and using pattern matching to recognize the words spoken.

Some voice recognition systems are speaker dependent, which means that the computer must be trained to identify an individual user's voice. Larger voice recognition systems use voice templates — multiple word patterns with male and female voices, as well as regional accents. These systems are speaker independent, because most users do not have to train the system to their individual speech patterns.

D. _____ software recognizes certain patterns that assist users by automating ordinary tasks, and changes how people interact with computers. Other intelligent agents, called _____, perform tasks on multiple remote computers before returning the results.

The agents in Microsoft's productivity software, called *wizards*, can be used for such diverse tasks as creating reports or brochures, drawing charts, developing presentations, and sending out party invitations. Network agents generally are considered more intelligent than wizards because they perform their work on remote computers without user prompts, and then bring the results back to the user.

E. _____ systems immerse a person in a simulated environment by surrounding the user with sight and sound.

Virtual reality (VR) software already is being employed by architects to let clients experience proposed construction or remodeling changes. VR has been used by scientists at NASA, surgeons, engineers, urban planners, and the U.S. Army. VR also is being used on the Internet for games, chat rooms, and more. Although still in its early stages, the increasing power of computers and the potential applications of VR have kept millions of dollars flowing into research.

F. _____ allows the same application to work on a variety of computers, so that a document created using Java can be run on Windows or a UNIX machine.

The differences among operating systems have made the development of cross-platform software a daunting task.

G. Most of the world's telephone network that connects distant places is digital and uses glass wires called _____.

With fiber-optic cable, data is converted into light pulses and transmitted by laser. Fiber-optic cable is more difficult to install than traditional copper cable. Nevertheless, fiber-optic cable offers higher volume, greater speed (about 10,000 times faster), lower error rate, increased security, and longer life. Japan plans to connect every home and business to fiber-optic cable by the year 2010.

The part of the telephone that is not digital, called the _____, is the section from a home or office to the local telephone exchange.

_____ (ISDN) converts the last mile to digital transmission through the modification of existing copper cable, increasing Internet access speeds for streaming video, interactivity, and real-time applications.

H. Advances in _____ technology have focused on using mobile telephones and handheld computers and devices. Cordless products with _____ technology, which allows wireless products to detect each other and communicate across a short distance, should flood the market.

Bluetooth™ (named for a 10ᵗʰ century Danish king who united Denmark and Norway) was developed by Ericsson in 1994 as a low-cost, powerful radio interface that could connect mobile phones to various devices. A Bluetooth™ enabled devices, such as personal computers, Internet appliances, handheld computers, cellular telephones, and fax machines.

II. The office of the future

Computers will empower workers by supporting collaboration, communication, and the ability to access and use information effectively.

A. _____ will be significantly improved by computers. _____ will be used for training in high risk professions, while _____ technologies will let people experience and evaluate new products before production.

Computer-aided design (CAD) technology uses a computer and special graphics software to assist in product planning. CAD eliminates laborious drafting and allows designers to dynamically change a product and then view the results of those changes. A related technology, called computer-aided engineering (CAE), uses computers to test product designs by simulating the effects of such factors as wind, temperature, weight, and stress on computer prototypes.

B. An interconnected work environment helps people work with and share information more effectively. Today, client server networks and e-mail are keeping coworkers connected. This trend will continue as technologies such as Internet telephones and video conferencing become increasingly common.

Many companies are posting internal web pages on internal networks called _____ . Employees use a Web browser to view pages on meetings, corporate polices, financial updates and more, just as they would view pages on the Web.

Exploring Windows

What does the future hold for Windows? According to Microsoft, prospective releases will incorporate some of the capabilities currently offered in Microsoft's other operating system, Windows NT. Many of the features of Windows, such as the graphical user interface and Plug-and-Play, also will be included in future versions of Windows NT, allowing new software applications to run on both platforms.

C. _____ is being created, used, and maintained in electronic form. Technologies such as _____ and _____ allow information to be converted from paper documents to electronic form and vice versa. _____ allow information to be converted from one format to another.

To cut down on paper, companies use _____ to send routine business documents.

_____ allows cutomers to order and pay for products and services over the Internet.

III. The home of the future

Technology is used in the home to save time and help people pursue their interests. Three technologies for the home are illustrated in Figure 14 on the next page.

A. New technologies allow people to _____ , which is the ability to work at home and communicate with the office using personal computers and communications channels.

   Using _____ , people can conduct meetings from home with video and computer technologies.

   _____ and _____ make it easy to share information from home.

   Telecommuting provides flexibility, allowing companies and employees to increase productivity and, at the same time, meet the needs of individual employees. Advantages of telecommuting include: reduced travel time, elimination of the need to travel in poor weather conditions, a convenient and comfortable work environment for disabled employees, and the ability to combine work and family responsibilities. Some cities have upgraded local communications channels to attract telecommuters.

B. The _____ of the future will provide integrated control of home systems, including security, environment, lighting, and sprinkler systems.

   Many existing home control systems are installed after the home was built and often consist of separate systems to control each set of devices. Chips are being designed, however, that will allow all appli-ances, lighting systems, and other home products to be net-worked together and controlled by a single system using a consistent set of commands. Bill Gates, founder of Microsoft, has 100 microcomputers built into his smart home. Residents and visitors wear pins that identify them and allow the house to adapt to their tastes —adjusting room temperatures, displaying favorite art images, playing personal music preferences, and gradually turning lights on and off as people enter and leave rooms.

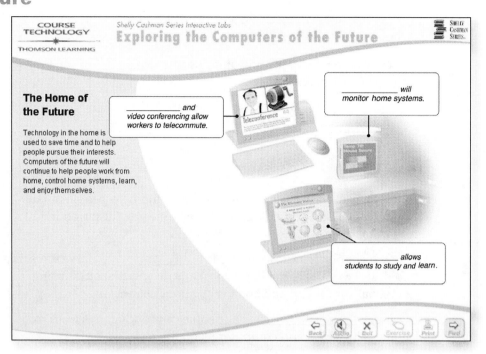

COURSE TECHNOLOGY

THOMSON LEARNING

Shelly Cashman Series Interactive Labs

Exploring the Computers of the Future

SHELLY CASHMAN SERIES.

The Home of the Future

Technology in the home is used to save time and to help people pursue their interests. Computers of the future will continue to help people work from home, control home systems, learn, and enjoy themselves.

_____ and video conferencing allow workers to telecommute.

_____ will monitor home systems.

_____ allows students to study and learn.

Back Audio Exit Exercise Print Fwd

Figure 14

C. The Internet and the World Wide Web are affecting education, as _____ allows students to take classes whenever they have time from home or workplace computers. University professors develop and distribute entire courses over the Internet.

_____ , also called _____ , helps students learn by using computers and instructional software delivered over the Internet or on CD-ROMs.

CAI software can be classified into three types:
- drill and practice (which uses a flash-card approach for review),
- tutorial (which uses text, graphics, and sound to teach concepts)
- simulation (which uses models by creating real-life situations).

Trade schools, colleges, and universities now offer distance learning classes.

D. Popular types of _____ software include arcade games, board games, and simulations. More powerful computers create interactive game with the illusion of reality.

In addition to gaming, computers entertain by _____ to other media and supporting activity.

Some games can be played in groups over a network such as the Internet. Hobbyists use computers for such diverse activities as designing quits and stained glass patterns, running model trains, organizing collections, and composing and playing music. You can read books or watch, and participate in, TV game shows on the Web.

E. The home computer of the future will enable people to
_____ home schedules and finances, and even
assist in home repair.

PC software is avialable to help you balance a checkbook, create a
household budget, and prepare tax returns. In addition, you can use
your PC to pay bills and perform other financial transactions, and
access a wealth of information and services.

F. _____ are computer-controlled devices that move
and react to feedback from the outside world.

Computers capable of performing human tasks will be seen
everywhere from hospitals to the home. The CareBot, a sophisticated
robot controlled by personal computer via radio signals, can fetch
drinks, help with homework, adjust room temperatures, monitor
home security, and even vacuum.

Exploring Your Computer

Consider some of the future advances in technology discussed in this lab. Which
do you think will have the greatest effect on the way you live and work? Why?
Which has the most appeal to you? Why? How do you think this technology
might be implemented in your computer?

Evaluating the Results

True/False

Instructions: Circle **T** if the statement is true or **F** if the statement is false.

T F 1. New production techniques and better quality materials are continually increasing the size of the components inside microprocessor chips.

T F 2. Virtual reality systems often use special accessories, such as goggles or gloves, to make the virtual environment seem real and allow the user to take actions within it.

T F 3. Most portable computers require a wireless connection to communicate.

T F 4. In the future, the trend toward interconnected work environments will continue, with technologies such as client-server networks, e-mail, Internet phones, and video conferencing becoming increasingly common.

T F 5. In the office of the future, the form in which information is stored and used will be determined primarily by computers.

Matching

Instructions: Write the letter of a description from the column on the right in front of each term in the column on the left.

_____ 1. Voice input

_____ 2. Handwriting recognition

_____ 3. Agents

_____ 4. Virtual reality

_____ 5. Cross-platform software

a. software that can be taught to recognize an individual's unique style of writing

b. software that uses computers to control production equipment

c. software that deals with values that are not precise and have a degree of uncertainty

d. software modules that exist within an application to facilitate work

e. software that allows users to enter data and issue commands with spoken words

f. software that creates an artificial environment that can be experienced by the computer user

g. software that will work with a variety of different computers and operating systems

Multiple Choice

Instructions: Circle the correct response.

1. What two types of software use pattern matching to convert what a user has input into a form that the computer understands?
   a. voice input software and agent software
   b. agent software and voice recognition software
   c. voice recognition software and handwriting recognition software
   d. handwriting recognition software and virtual reality software

2. Which of the following is not an advantage that fiber-optic cables have over copper cables?
   a. larger capacity
   b. easier installation
   c. increased speed
   d. clearer signals

3. Like cellular phones, wireless computers use what technology to communicate without a physical connection?
   a. radio frequency (RF)
   b. microwave (MW)
   c. laser-beam (LB)
   d. infrared (IR)

4. What is computer-aided design (CAD)?
   a. technology that uses computers to control production equipment and scheduling
   b. technology that integrates the entire manufacturing process using computers
   c. technology that allows computer users to alter the motherboard and peripherals
   d. technology that lets people experience and evaluate products before production

5. In the home of the future, technologies such as fax machines, e-mail, and video conferencing will help people most in which of the following areas?
   a. telecommuting
   b. control of home systems
   c. entertainment
   d. home management

Fill in the Blanks

Instructions: Place the correct word(s) in the blank in each sentence.

1. A(n) _____ is a credit-card-sized piece of plastic with an embedded microprocessor chip that can store and process information and transactions.

2. _____ systems often use special accessories, such as goggles or gloves, to make the environment seem real and allow the user to take actions within it.

3. _____ are a new type of wire made of glass that can transmit an almost infinite amount of information.

4. _____ programs allow paper documents to be converted into electronic form, and vice versa.

5. _____ allows people to attend meetings and communicate face to face while at separate locations.

Examining the Issues

Examining the **Issues**

1. As tuition costs rise, students increasingly are aware of the other financial burdens — books, supplies, room, board, and so on — associated with a college education. In the future, however, they may face an additional expense: mandatory computers. Already, one university requires that entering freshmen purchase a specific laptop computer at a cost of about $2,000. Another university insists that every student have uninterrupted, 24-hour access to some kind of personal computer. Students at both schools have protested the new mandates, claiming the additional expense will make college unaffordable for some students and threaten the economic diversity of the student population. Are the computer policies of these schools justified? Why or why not? What impact would personal computer requirements have on the student body? Why?

2. One of the strongest high school memories for many people is dissecting a frog in biology class. In the future, however, virtual reality software may replace the scalpel and frog cadaver. Programs such as Virtual Frog and MacInvertebrate approximate real dissections as students use tweezers on the computer screen to place virtually dissected tissues in a petri dish. The experience may be enhanced with color-coded organs, cheers for correct identifications, and even movies of the digestive, reproductive, and skeletal systems. While the virtual reality software has won the praise of squeamish students and animal-rights activists, the National Association of Biology Teachers continues to favor real dissections for instruction. Should a virtual reality experience take the place of genuine dissections in high school classes? Why or why not?

Investigating World
the

1. Visit a software vendor and do one of the following:

   - Try out a software application that includes an agent or wizard, such as Microsoft Word or Microsoft Excel. For what purpose is the wizard used? What are the advantages of using a wizard? What are the disadvantages? Is the final result produced by the wizard more or less attractive, creative, or distinctive than what you could have done on your own? Why? Would you be more likely to buy an application with or without a wizard? Why?

   - Find at least two different software applications that can be used to assist with similar home accounting tasks, such as balancing checkbooks, making household budgets, or preparing tax returns. What is the name of each application? What is the cost? What are the hardware require-ments? If possible, test each one , performing the same tasks. Which one is easier to use? Why? Does either application offer more capabilities? What are they? On the basis of your examination, which software, if any, would you be most inclined to purchase? Why?

2. Volunteer to help out in a primary or secondary school class while it is using computer-aided instruction (CAI). What software is being used? What is it trying to teach? What type of software (drill and practice, tutorial, or simulation) is it? Could the same topic be taught more effectively using a different type of software? Why or why not? Could the topic be taught better by a teacher? Why? How do the students respond to CAI? From your observation, what are the advantages of CAI? What are the disadvantages? In general, are your feelings about computer-aided instruction positive or negative? Why?

Understanding Multimedia

Summarizing the Lab

15

Instructions: Use the *Understanding Multimedia* interactive lab to complete the following outline.

I. What is multimedia?

_____ refers to any computer program that combines media elements such as text, graphics, animations, audio, and video. The basic elements of multimedia are shown in Figure 15.

COURSE TECHNOLOGY
THOMSON LEARNING

Shelly Cashman Series Interactive Labs
Understanding Multimedia

SHELLY CASHMAN SERIES.

Multimedia Elements

2. _____ is sound that has been digitized and stored for replay.

Multimedia refers to any computer program that combines:

→ Text

1. _____ is used to provide basic information and hypertext links.

5. _____ refers to the movement of graphics on the screen to illustrate concepts or simulate movement of connected parts.

3. _____ allow you to show information rather than just describing it, and to communicate without the barrier or language.

4. _____ is made up of photographic images displayed to simulate motion in real time.

Back   Audio   Exit   Exercise   Print   Fwd

Figure 15

II. Interactivity

The most distinguishing features of multimedia are its
_____ and its _____. A multimedia
application that accepts input from the user is called interactive multimedia. Interacting with multimedia applications usually requires a
mouse or other pointing device, which is used to choose what material is
presented and in what order.

Hyperlinks can be clicked to access information within a multimedia
application in a nonlinear fashion. Hyperlinks can be _____ ,
which are text-based, or _____ , which are based on
graphics or other media. Hypertext links sometimes are known as
hotwords.

III. Multimedia elements

In multimedia applications, there usually are some on-screen text
displays along with hyperlinks that when clicked might:

- Playback an audio recording
- Display a graphic
- Playback a video demonstration
- Begin an animated simulation

A. Audio components

Multimedia PCs contain _____ that allow the audio used in a
multimedia application to be recorded or played back. A sound card
is a _____ with processors that provide both audio
input and output.

Using _____ with a sound card allows audio signals
to be combined and recording and playback levels to be modified.

Sound is a powerful informational tool, whether used alone or
accompanied by other types of media. The sounds of a beating heart,
a native French speaker, or a symphony can be conveyed well only
with audio capability. An actor's narration added to the text of a
Shakespearean play can enhance understanding of the work.

Audio is sound that has been digitized and stored for replay. Two
factors determine the quality of the sound heard when an audio file
is played: _____ and _____ (in bits). In general, the
higher the sound quality, the larger the audio file.

Exploring Windows

Windows includes a Media Player to allow you to play audio, video, or animation files — even your favorite music CDs! The Media Player also allows you to control the settings for multimedia hardware devices such as speakers. To start the Media Player, click the Start button, point to Programs on the Start menu, and point to Accessories on the submenu. Point to Multimedia on the Accessories submenu and click Media Player. Choose the appropriate device (CD Audio, Video for Windows, and so on) and enjoy the show!

B. Graphics

_____ allow information to be shown, rather than just described. Pictures also communicate without the barrier of language. People are more visually oriented than ever before —witness the popularity of television, movies, and highly visual magazines.

A graphic is a _____ image that can be displayed by a computer. Graphics can be purchased in clip art collections or created with a drawing software package. Photographs can be digitized with a scanner, captured with a digital camera, or purchased on CD-ROMs.

The graphics used in multimedia range from simple two-dimensional (2-D) drawings to intricate, photorealistic, three-dimensional (3-D) images.

1. The two dimensions of 2-D graphics are _____ and _____. In multimedia applications, 2-D graphics often serve as objects that can be selected as hyperlinks.

2. 3-D graphics have the added dimension of _____. 3-D graphics are created using specialized software that shows greater levels of detail and makes images more realistic.

C. Video

Video is made up of photographic images displayed at rates of up to _____ per second to simulate motion in real time. Video is used widely in multimedia applications designed for training.

Multimedia PCs have video capture cards and display adapters, which can be used to record and play back video clips.

Like audio, video must be converted from _____ to _____ to be used by a computer. Digital video files are very large. These files must be reduced in size to be accessed and managed by a computer. The process of reducing the size of a file and later expanding it for viewing is called _____.

Video compression takes advantage of the fact that only a small portion of the image changes from frame to frame. A compression program might store the first reference frame and then store only the changes from one frame to the next. The Moving Pictures Expert Group (MPEG) has developed compression methods that can reduce the size of video files up to 95 percent, while retaining near-television quality.

D. Animations

_____ refers to the movement of graphics on the screen. Animations can illustrate concepts more vividly than text or still graphics. An animation showing a piston valve opening and closing as it moves up and down provides a better depiction of how an internal combustion engine works than still pictures and a written description.

Three types of animations are:

1. _____ are similar to 2-D graphics, except that they have movement.

2. _____ provide the added dimension of perspective. 3-D animations can simulate the movement of connected parts. Even simple 3-D animations are created from detailed, computer-generated models and take a long time to create.

3. _____ uses computer-generated 3-D animation to simulate whole, interactive worlds. Interactive 3-D animations are created using _____ , which stands for _____.

IV. Multimedia and the CD-ROM

_____ technology has played an important role in the development of multimedia. Multimedia files often are too large to be stored practically on floppy disks. A CD-ROM, however, can store about the same amount of data as _____ floppy disks.

CD-ROM drives with slower transfer rates often fail to fully integrate audio and video. Quad-speed or higher CD-ROM drives are needed to ensure smooth playback of multimedia files.

CD-ROMs have made the development and delivery of powerful multimedia applications possible and practical.

V. Multimedia personal computers

A _____ has specific hardware and software components used to input, process, and output the media used in multimedia applications. of standards developed by several companies in the computer industry. The most recent level is _____.

MPCs are classified according to two standards:

- The _____ established the MPC levels

- _____and _____ set up the PC classifications.

Components for which MPC Level 3 standards set minimum requirements are:

- _____
- _____
- _____
- _____
- _____
- _____
- _____

Exploring Your Computer

Does your computer have any components of a multimedia PC? For instance, does it have a CD-ROM drive? Does it have a sound card and speakers? Are the speakers built into the computer or are they attached by a cable? Could your computer be considered an MPC Level 2 or 3 multimedia computer?

VI. Uses of multimedia

Multimedia is used in business and education for training, marketing, reference, entertainment, and more.

A. One application of multimedia is _____ , which is used to teach specific skills on the spot, instead of having employees attend outside workshops.

Interactive training software, called courseware, can be distributed by CD-ROM or shared over a network.

B. Many businesses use multimedia to _____ and sell products and to create exciting _____. Multimedia software demos can be mailed as advertisements. The Internet is another way companies are delivering multimedia marketing and advertising materials.

C. Many public places have computerized reference centers, called _____ , which are used to find specific information or browse through choices. Information kiosks often use _____ monitors that allow users to make selections by touching the appropriate area on the screen.

D. Many books, magazines, and reference texts are available in an interactive multimedia format. The pages of an electronic book are turned by clicking icons. Multimedia magazines use many types of media to convey information.

_____ is a complete CD-ROM encyclopedia that uses graphics, animation, audio, and video to accompany the text. Digital texts usually contain hyperlinks to additional information.

E. Interactive multimedia computer games use _____ , _____ , and _____ to create a realistic, entertaining game. Often, the game simulates a real or fictitious world, in which the player takes the role of a character and has control of what happens. Some new multimedia products provide edutainment, an experience meant to be both educational and entertaining.

VII. Authoring multimedia applications

Multimedia applications are created using _____ . You build the application by _____ objects and media elements onto the screen.

Many authoring programs allow you to create applications that can be viewed on the _____ .

Different multimedia authoring packages use different metaphors or analogies to help create a multimedia application. Popular multimedia authoring packages include ToolBook, which uses a book metaphor; Authorware, which uses a flowchart metaphor; and Director, which uses a theater metaphor.

Evaluating the Results

True/False

Instructions: Circle **T** if the statement is true or **F** if the statement is false.

T F 1. Multimedia hyperlinks can be hypertext links, which are text-based, or hypermedia links, which are based on graphics or other media.

T F 2. Video must be converted from digital to analog to be used by a computer.

T F 3. Digital video files are very small and must be expanded in size so the computer can access and manage the files.

T F 4. Simple 3-D animations, like a bouncing ball, are produced with basic paint programs and take very little time to create.

T F 5. A multimedia personal computer (MPC) has specific hardware and software components used to input, process, and output the media used in multimedia applications.

Matching

Instructions: Write the letter of a description from the column on the right in front of each term in the column on the left.

____ 1. Computer-based training (CBT)

____ 2. Marketing and advertising

____ 3. Information kiosks

____ 4. Encyclopedia and references

____ 5. Multimedia games

a. located in many public places to help people find specific facts or browse through choices

b. many companies are using the Internet to deliver these multimedia materials

c. used to record daily occurrences, events, meetings, and reminders

d. often simulate a real or fictitious world in which users play the role of a character

e. compares a company's sales to its expenses and calculates net profit or loss

f. multimedia versions usually contain hyperlinks to more information, such as definitions or video

g. used to teach specific skills on the spot, instead of having employees attend outside workshops

Multiple Choice

Instructions: Circle the correct response.

1. What are the most distinguishing features of multimedia?
   a. its reliance on a single medium and its inactivity
   b. its simplicity and its need for a variety of input devices
   c. its combination of media elements and its interactivity
   d. its banality and its insignificant system requirements

2. What are the two dimensions of 2-D graphics?
   a. width and height
   b. height and depth
   c. depth and weight
   d. weight and width

3. What do sampling rate and resolution (in bits) determine?
   a. the rate at which text files are transferred from memory
   b. the quality of the sound heard when an audio file is played
   c. the clarity of an animation or video file when it is decompressed
   d. the time it takes to empty a bag of potato chips at a fraternity party

4. Why has CD-ROM technology played an important role in the development of multimedia?
   a. the durability of CD-ROMs has made it possible to transport multimedia applications anywhere
   b. the large storage capacity of CD-ROMs has made multimedia applications possible and practical
   c. the adaptability of CD-ROMs has allowed users to make changes to multimedia applications
   d. the availability of CD-ROMs has made interactive multimedia applications viable in any setting

5. For what components does the MPC Level 3 set minimum requirements?
   a. RAM and CPU
   b. hard drive and CD-ROM drive
   c. input and output devices
   d. all of the above

Fill in the Blanks

Instructions: Place the correct word(s) in the blank in each sentence.

1. _____ refers to any computer program that combines media elements such as text, graphics, animations, audio, and video.

2. Multimedia PCs contain _____ , which are circuit boards housing processors that provide both audio input and output.

3. _____ uses computer-generated 3-D animations to simulate whole, interactive worlds.

4. Multimedia personal computers often are referred to by their
_____ , which is a set of hardware and software standards
developed by several companies in the computer industry.

5. Information kiosks often use _____ monitors that let selections be
made by contacting the appropriate area on the screen.

Examining the Issues

1. Designing a multimedia application includes developing a project script
that provides a written record of how various media elements will be used.
For each frame in a multimedia application, the script describes the text,
graphics, animation, audio, and interactivity (what users will do and the
application response). Some guidelines for effective multimedia
applications are:

   - Know the audience (tailor the application to meet users' needs).

   - Give users control (allow users to choose their own course).

   - Immerse the user (recreate tasks users must perform).

   - Require interaction (ask questions and provide feedback).

   - Review concepts (incorporate self-building exercises).

   - Engage the user (make the application attractive and appealing to the
   eye and ear).

   Write a short script for a multimedia application on a subject of your choice.
   Assume the application will use at least ten frames. Include descriptions of
   the multimedia elements in each frame.

2. Multimedia applications, particularly in the form of computer-based
training (CBT), are assuming an increasingly important role in education.
Advocates claim multimedia applications make learning more interesting,
allow students to perform in a risk-free environment, provide instant feedback, and appeal to different learning styles. CBT offers reduced learning
time, self-paced study, one-on-one interaction, decreased learning costs,
and unique instructional experiences. Some supporters propose radically
different classrooms with multimedia applications providing the bulk of
the learning experience. Instead of being a sage on the stage, the teacher
would guide on the side, circulating among students and offering
individual help. What advantages of CBT are most important? Why? What
are the disadvantages of CBT? For what subjects is CBT most appropriate?
Why? Will the radical vision of a classroom dedicated to CBT ever be
realized? Why or why not?

Investigating the World

1. The development of interactive multimedia applications involves the use of multimedia authoring software. These programs combine text, graphics, animation, audio, and video and incorporate interactivity into a finished multimedia application. Three popular multimedia authoring programs are ToolBook (from Asymetrix Corporation), Authorware Professional (from Macromedia Inc.), and Director (from Macromedia Inc.). Each program uses a different metaphor (comparison) to make authoring easier: ToolBook uses a book metaphor, Authorware uses a flowchart metaphor, and Director uses a theater metaphor. Visit a software vendor and ask for a demonstration of a multimedia authoring program. What are the system requirements? How compatible is the program with other applications? Is the program easy to use? Why or why not? What functions does it perform? What technical support is offered? How good is the application developed?

2. A broad category of multimedia reference books is how-to guides. These interactive applications help people deal with tasks they face in their daily lives. The Reader's Digest Complete Do-It-Yourself Guide offers hundreds of home repair how-to tips. Animated tours also are provided that show ways to a beautiful home. The Williams-Sonoma Guide to Good Cooking is a multi-media cookbook. In addition to more than 1,000 recipes, the CD-ROM includes a search function that locates dishes with specific characteristics, a menu planner, and video tips. Microsoft's Automap Streets Plus is a multi-media travel guide. Information is offered on hotels, restaurants, museums, and tourist centers. Road maps show addresses throughout the United States. Visit a software vendor or resource center and try a multimedia how-to guide. What information does it provide? How easy is it to use? What advantages does it have over a printed guide? What are the disadvantages? How could the guide be improved?

Keeping Your Computer Virus Free

Summarizing the Lab

16

Instructions: Use the *Keeping Your Computer Virus* Free interactive lab to complete the following outline.

I. What is a computer virus?

A computer virus is a _____ designed to spread copies of itself to computer systems without detection. Once spread, it causes the infected computer systems to perform unwanted actions.

A survey of American companies with more than 200 personal computers showed that over 60 percent had suffered at least one viral attack. Because two of the major sources of viruses — illegally copied software and free software — are used more commonly by small companies and private PC users, the total percentage of PCs affected by viruses may be much higher.

> Exploring Your Computer
>
> Have you ever experienced problems with a virus on your computer? If so, were you able to successfully remove the virus? Is there a virus protection program, such as IBM AntiVirus, McAfee VirusScan, Cheyenne InocuLan, or Norton AntiVirus, running on your computer?

II. The process of virus infection

Viruses secretly invade a computer via a _____ or _____.

A. Software that has a virus attached is aclled a _____ .

The three main types of viruses are named after the places they hide: _____ , _____ , and _____ .

1. A _____ replaces the startup code on a disk with a modified version, which is loaded into memory when the computer is booted (started).

   From memory, the virus can infect any disk used by the computer.

2. A _____ inserts virus code into program files, where it intercepts the program's execution and takes control of the computer system.

   Viruses usually infect executable files, rather than data files, on a computer system.

3. A _____ is disguised to look like a legitimate program and is launched by an unsuspecting user, believing it is useful software.

   Frequently found on bulletin boards, these programs may appear to be utilities or games.

B. Once a virus has infected a computer, it uses the computer's resources to secretly _____ of itself, sometimes attaching copies to new data files.

   Viruses also copy themselves onto _____ that is inserted into the computer's drive. Any computers that run the infected disk also will become infected. Viruses can multiply _____ as users share infected files.

   School computer labs can be a particularly fertile breeding ground for viruses. One student with an infected application program disk can spread a virus to several laboratory computers, which in turn contaminate other students' application software.

C. Viruses are designed to become active at a specific point.

   The three main categories of viruses, based on the actions that trigger them, are illustrated in Figure 16.

1. A _____ is a virus that stops duplicating and becomes active when a certain date registers on the computer system's clock.

   Time bombs are sometimes a legitimate part of leased software. When the software is run, the program checks the date. If the date is past the terminal date of the lease, the software does not work.

   Halloween, April Fool's Day, and Friday the 13th are favorite days for viral attacks. Some companies routinely back up all software before these dates.

Figure 16

2. A _____ is triggered by the appearance or disappearance of a certain kind of data.

   Logic bombs are activated by the appearance or disappearance of certain data. For example, a disgruntled employee could insert a logic bomb that would go off if the employee's name is removed from the payroll file.

3. A _____ is a virus-like program that creates copies of itself continuously until the computer system is overloaded and stops working.

   Unlike a virus, worms do not need a host program. Worm programs enter a system through a computer network. In 1988, a worm created by a Cornell graduate student entered the Internet, affecting about 6,000 computers. A spokesperson claimed the worm cost NASA over 140 person-years of labor to eradicate.

III. Effects on the computer

A benign virus may announce itself with _____ on the computer screen.

A more malicious virus may cause the computer to behave erratically or _____ of e-mails, overwhelming a server.

Many viruses corrupt or destroy valuable _____ .

A virus program can be just a few lines of code inserted in a legitimate program. When the program is run, the virus code can display an irritating comment, interrupt processing, or delete data from the hard disk.

IV. Detecting and removing viruses

Several steps can be taken to detect and remove viruses.

A. First, restart the computer using a _____ , which is a startup disk that is known to be clean.

A virus removal program sometimes can be used to delete virus code from a program. If the infection is too severe, however, a rescue disk insures the virus has been eradicated and programs can be reinstalled from the original disks.

B. Next, run an _____ program to look for program fragments that change boot sectors or the computer's operating system, which usually are _____ files.

> ### Exploring Windows
> New anti-virus programs are available that take advantage of the features Windows offers. Some of the these anti-virus programs for Windows are:
> - Data Fellows's F-PROT Professional
> - McAfee's VirusScan
> - Symantec's Norton AntiVirus

Some anti-virus programs are designed to be run periodically, while others continually monitor system activity. Examples of anti-virus programs include Norton AntiVirus and Microsoft Anti-Virus. But, buyer beware — soon after a popular, inexpensive anti-virus program called Flu Shot IV came on the market, it was infected with a virus and offered for free on computer bulletin boards.

Anti-virus programs scan memory and files for _____ , which are patterns of code from known viruses.

To avoid reinfection, every floppy disk used on a computer system should be checked with an anti-virus program. The search for virus signatures is fast; however, it is important to remember that only viruses with known signatures can be detected.

Anti-virus programs also can protect files against future infection by _____ , which involves recording file size and creation data so changes can be detected.

Using the recorded information, the vaccine program can tell if a virus program has tampered with the program file. Some anti-virus programs use a checksum — a value calculated by adding all the bytes in a file — which is reviewed each time the file is accessed to make sure the file has not been changed.

C. To prevent virus infection, you should:

1. Install _____ to automatically check new files for viruses.

2. Use an _____ to scan disks for viruses before accessing them.

3. Check _____ for viruses before running them.

4. Be especially careful when _____ software from the Web.

Exploring Online

Many Web sites offer information on anti-virus software and advice for protecting your computer against viruses. Some of these are:

- Data Fellows's Computer Virus Information page
- Stiller Research
- Symantec Anti-Virus Reference Center

To obtain more details on viruses and anti-virus programs, visit the Exploring Computers Web page (www.scsite.com/expl.htm) and click Viruses.

Evaluating the Results

True/False

Instructions: Circle **T** if the statement is true or **F** if the statement is false.

T F 1. Once a virus has infected a computer, it uses the computer's resources to secretly spread copies of itself.

T F 2. Viruses cannot copy themselves onto floppy disks inserted into the computer's disk drive.

T F 3. Worm programs wait for a specific event, and so are much more complicated than time bombs or logic bombs.

T F 4. Virus signature files rarely need to be updated.

T F 5. Inoculating a file involves recording a file's size and creation date so an anti-virus program can detect if the file is changed by a virus.

Matching

Instructions: Write the letter of a description from the column on the right in front of each term in the column on the left.

_____ 1. Boot-sector virus

_____ 2. File virus

_____ 3. Trojan horse virus

_____ 4. Time bomb

_____ 5. Logic bomb

a. intercepts execution when a legitimate program file is run and takes control of the system

b. replaces startup code on a disk with a modified version

c. repeatedly copies itself in memory or on a disk drive until no space remains

d. is disguised to look like a legitimate program, frequently found on bulletin boards

e. becomes active when a certain date registers on the computer system's clock

f. looks for program fragments that change the computer's operating system

g. triggered when a particular event occurs, such as an employee being terminated

Multiple Choice

Instructions: Circle the correct response.

1. What does a virus do after invading a computer system?
   a. it takes control of the computer system
   b. it hides, waiting for a specific event to occur
   c. it damages hardware and peripheral devices
   d. it sets up permanent residence in memory

2. What type of virus is loaded into memory when the computer is started?
   a. boot-sector virus
   b. file virus
   c. program virus
   d. Trojan horse virus

3. Michelangelo's virus, which becomes active on March 6 (Michelangelo's birthday), is an example of what type of virus?
   a. logic bomb
   b. worm
   c. time bomb
   d. vaccine

4. What effect might a virus have on a computer?
   a. unexpected messages appear on the computer screen
   b. the computer behaves erratically or freezes
   c. valuable data is corrupted or destroyed
   d. all of the above

5. Which of the following is not a step that should be followed to prevent infection by a computer virus?
   a. install virus protection software
   b. use an anti-virus program
   c. check new programs for viruses after running them
   d. be especially careful with software posted to computer bulletin boards

Fill in the Blanks

Instructions: Place the correct word(s) in the blank in each sentence.

1. A(n) _____ is a program designed to spread copies of itself without detection to computer systems.

2. A(n) _____ is a virus-like program that continuously copies itself until the computer system is overloaded and stops working.

3. If a virus is found, the computer should be restarted using a(n) _____ to ensure that the computer is running without any viruses in memory.

4. A(n) _____ looks for program fragments that change boot sectors of the computer's operating system, which are normally read-only files.

5. Anti-virus programs scan memory and files for patterns of code from known viruses, called _____ .

Examining the Issues

1. Computer viruses first appeared in the mid-1980s. Since then, viruses have ruined hospital records, wiped out bank registers, obliterated programs in thousands of personal computers, and cost businesses and government enormous amounts of money and numbers of work hours. Although a few viruses are created for personal gain or revenge against an organization, most viruses are launched without a specific target. Why do you think people create computer viruses? What, if anything, can be done to stop this malicious mischief?

2. In a famous case, Robert Morris was found guilty of infecting a computer network with a virus that damaged data and files for more than 6,000 users. Morris's sentence was 400 hours of community service, a three year probation, and a $10,000 fine. Some people feel this sentence was too lenient, given the extent of the harm the virus caused. Others believe Morris actually did the network a favor by demonstrating the limitations of its security system. Was the punishment appropriate? Why or why not? Would this punishment serve as a deterrent to other potential computer criminals?

Investigating the World

1. Of the thousands of known viruses, some have become particularly well known, either because of their effects on computer systems or as a result of their impact on computer users. Famous computer viruses include the ARPAnet data virus, the Scores virus, the Bell Labs virus, the brain virus, the Israeli virus, the Lehigh virus, the MacMag virus, the Stoned virus, the Friday the 13th virus, and the Michelangelo virus. Using a library, the Web, or another research facility, prepare a brief report on any three viruses. What type of virus was each? How was it triggered? What was its effect? What impact did it have on computer users? Was the creator of the virus ever discovered? If so, how?

2. As with other software, when purchasing anti-virus programs it is important to buy software that suits your needs. Visit a computer vendor and find at least two anti-virus programs. What is the name of each? How much does each cost? With which type of computer (or operating system) does each work? How easy are they to use? How does each detect a virus? How many viruses can they detect? When was each last updated? Will there be future updates? If so, how much will the updates cost? After answering these questions, which program would you be more likely to buy? Why?

Designing a Database

Summarizing the Lab 17

Instructions: Use the *Designing a Database* interactive lab to complete the following outline.

I. What is a database?

A database is a way of _____ a large amount of data to provide easy access.

Effective data management involves data integrity or data accuracy (assuring the reliability of the source and entry of data), data security (protecting data to keep it from being misused or lost), and data maintenance (keeping data current).

Exploring Windows

Most personal computer database software applications have versions that take advantage of the features offered by Windows. Some of the database packages with versions designed for Windows are:

- Borland Visual dBASE
- Claris FileMaker Pro
- Corel Paradox 7
- Lotus Approach
- Microsoft Access
- Microsoft Visual FoxPro

Each similar item in a database is stored as a _____ .
Data within each record is divided into areas called

_____ .

A file is a collection of related data or information. Files are made up of records, which are structured groups of related facts. The individual facts within each record are called fields. The same fields are used in each record in a file.

Data typically is stored as an isolated set called a
_____ , an independent file that contains all the
information necessary to process the records in that file.

Flat files usually are designed for a single application. All the records in a
flat file have the same format (the same fields and the same data types).

A database allows users to access and relate data across _____ ,
rather than restricting a search to a single file.

Because database files are related, records can be processed using information from more than one file. Users can draw information from a database for a variety of purposes in different formats.

Databases offer several advantages over flat files.

- Reduced data redundancy — In a database, shared data elements are
  stored in a single location.

- Improved data integrity — With a database, data is updated in a
  single location, so it is more likely to be accurate.

- Easier reporting — A database allows data to be extracted from
  multiple files at one time.

- Improved data security — One plan can establish different levels of
  access to the information in a database.

- Reduced development time — In a database, additional data can be
  accommodated by adding new attributes to existing files.

II. Types of databases

The four main categories of database structure are shown in Figure 17.

A. In a _____ database, data is organized in a series
   of parent-child relationships.

   Because a child record can have only one parent, if a child record
   belongs in two different families _____ must be
   placed in each one.

   Hierarchical databases are the oldest form of database organization.
   Data stored on lower levels of the hierarchy is accessed through the
   higher levels. All data relationships are established when the hierarchical database is created. As a result, adding new fields to the
   database requires the redefinition of the entire database. Because
   data relationships are predefined, however, access to and updating of
   data is very fast.

B. A _____ database is similar to a hierarchical database except that each child record can have more than one parent.

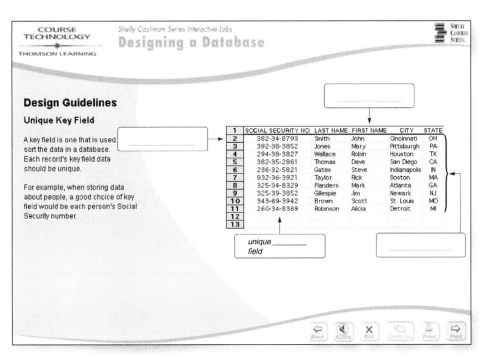

Figure 17

Sharing a child record eliminates _____ and increases _____ .

In a network database, parent and child records are referred to as _____ and _____ .

An owner and its one or more associated members is called a set (or owner-coupled set). A member can be accessed through any of its owners. Like a hierarchical database, data relationships must be established before the database is used and must be redefined if fields are added or modified.

C. A _____ database links data in multiple files using a single field that is common to each file.

Databases containing different _____ can be accessed easily once they are linked using a common field. New fields can be added to one database without affecting the others.

In a relational database, data is organized in tables (called relations), which are further divided into rows (called tuples) and fields (called attributes). Relational databases offer more flexibility than hierarchical or network databases; because data relationships are not predefined, attributes can be added without having to redefine the entire database. Yet, its more complex software requires more powerful computers to provide acceptable performance.

D. An _____ database stores objects, which are items that contain data and the actions that can be taken on that data.

Object-oriented databases are the most adaptable type of database. In hierarchical, network, and relational databases, the same fields are used for each record in a file. A company using one of these database types might need two files to calculate its weekly payroll: one with an hourly rate field for employees paid by the hour, and a second with an annual salary field for salaried employees. Because it allows variations of a single record type, however, records in an object-oriented database can contain many different methods to compute weekly pay.

Exploring Online

Several sites on the Internet provide a comprehensive glossary of database terms, and tips and tricks for good database design. Some excellent database resources on the Web include:

- Data Warehouse Glossary
- University of Massachusetts Database Systems Laboratory
- Association for Computing Machinery's Special Interest Group on Management of Data

For more information on designing a database, visit the Exploring Computers Web page (www.scsite.com/expl.htm) and click Database.

III. Accessing a database

_____ a database involves entering a request that specifies which data to display.

Two ways to make a query are:

A. _____ enables the user to build a query step by step. A list of database fields is presented, and the user enters _____ into one or more of the fields. As the user narrows the qualifiers, only the data that matches the choices is displayed.

Users can enter simple expressions in a field (such as Jones in a LASTNAME field to find people whose last names are Jones) or create expressions in a field using relational operators (such as >30 in an AGE field to find people older than thirty). Criteria can be combined using the logical operators, NOT, AND, and OR (for example, Jones in a LASTNAME field AND >30 in an AGE field to find people named Jones who are older than thirty).

B. A _____ enables users to describe what data they wish to access using English-like phrases, following the syntax of the query language. _____ is the most widely-used query language.

The American National Standards Institute issued standards for SQL in 1987. Today, most database software has incorporated SQL.

Three operations are used to query a relational database: select (which chooses certain records), project (which specifies the fields, or attributes, that appear on the query output), and join (which combines two files or relations).

IV. Database features

Features in a database management system that help to maintain data include: _____ , _____ , _____ , and _____ .

A. The _____ defines how data in the database is organized into fields and helps ensure new data is entered correctly.

Because it contains the structures and specifications for the database, a data dictionary must be carefully designed and documented.

B. _____ provide maintenance features, such as copying or deleting records and monitoring the database's performance.

C. _____ features enable the database creators to set various levels of access privileges that determine how different users can interact with the data.

Without some type of access security, data in a database is more subject to unauthorized access than data in a decentralized system of individual files.

D. The _____ feature tracks changes made to the database. Changes are recorded in a _____ , which can be used to reconstruct data in the event of accident or malfunction and to reveal patterns of database use.

V. Design guidelines

Carefully designed database files can make it easy for the user to query and report on database information. For relational databases, a process called normalization is used to organize data into the most efficient and logical file relationships.

Designing an efficient and powerful database can be done by following some simple guidelines.

A. Designing a database _____ first helps you determine how the data should be organized before tackling the details.

Designing a Database

B. A _____ is used to sort the data in a database. Each record's key field should be _____ .

C. Data that can be derived from existing fields in the database is _____ and can be eliminated.

D. If any items need to be referred to separately, it is best to keep them in _____ .

E. Adding a _____ , or a value that is usually the same for a particular field, can greatly reduce the time it takes to add new data.

Although formal rules do not exist for designing flat files, the same common sense guidelines can be applied to both databases and flat files.

Evaluating the Results

True/False

Instructions: Circle **T** if the statement is true or **F** if the statement is false.

T F 1. A flat file enables users to access and relate data across multiple files.

T F 2. Query by example, or QBE, enables the user to build a query step by step.

T F 3. A log can reveal patterns of database use and provide a data trail that can be used to reconstruct a database in the event of an accident or malfunction.

T F 4. Each record's key field data should be the same as every other record's key field data.

T F 5. Any data that can be derived from existing fields in a database should be entered again in a separate field.

Matching

Instructions: Write the letter of a description from the column on the right in front of each term in the column on the left.

_____ 1. Query language

_____ 2. Data dictionary

_____ 3. Utility program

_____ 4. Data security

_____ 5. Data recovery

a. enables users to describe the data they wish to access using English-like phrases

b. combines items containing data with actions that can be taken on the data

c. links multiple files using a single field

d. tracks changes made to the database and records changes in a log

e. enables the database creators to set different levels of access privileges

f. provides maintenance features such as copying or deleting records

g. defines how data in the database is organized into fields

Designing a Database

Multiple Choice

Instructions: Circle the correct response.

1. Each similar item in a database is stored as what?
   a. a file
   b. a record
   c. a field
   d. a relation

2. In what type of database is data organized in a series of parent-child relationships?
   a. hierarchical
   b. network
   c. relational
   d. object-oriented

3. In what type of database can new fields be added without affecting the other fields?
   a. hierarchical
   b. network
   c. relational
   d. all of the above

4. What helps to ensure that new data is entered into the database correctly?
   a. a data dictionary
   b. utility programs
   c. data security
   d. data recovery

5. Which of the following is not a guideline for designing an efficient and powerful database?
   a. start on paper
   b. use a unique key field
   c. choose default values
   d. maximize data redundancy

Fill in the Blanks

Instructions: Place the correct word(s) in the blank in each sentence.

1. A(n) _____ is a collection of related files and a way of storing a large amount of data to allow easy access.

2. Data typically is stored in an independent, isolated set called a(n) _____ .

3. In a network database, parent and child records are referred to as _____ and members.

4. A(n) _____ database stores items containing data and the actions that can be taken on that data.

5. _____ is the most widely used query language.

Examining the Issues

1. Imagine if, instead of using a central database, your school used a flat file system to handle student records. Basic data (such as your name, address, and telephone number) may be kept in a central office file; financial data would be kept in the school business office file; data concerning your grades may be kept in files by individual instructors; and data on the credits you have earned would be in department and central office files. What would be the disadvantages of this type of system? What might be the advantages?

2. Data security is an important part of managing data. With a database system, data security often involves setting varying access levels for different groups of people. Access levels might include: (1) no access at all; (2) data can be viewed but not changed; (3) some data can be changed but not all; and (4) total access with no restraints. Consider your student file. In addition to your name, address, and grades, this file may contain information on your ethnicity, gender, family, financial status, health, extra-curricular activities, disciplinary record, and so on. Using this file as an example, which of the four levels of access privileges would you give to each of the following groups: you, other students, faculty, administration, and outside organizations. Why?

Investigating World the

1. Automobile dealers often use databases that contain information both about cars in their own inventories and cars in the inventories of related dealers. Most libraries use computerized databases to keep track of their own collections and books in neighboring libraries. Law enforcement agencies use databases to store data on past criminal activity. Visit one of these organizations or another organization that uses a database, and interview the person in charge of the organization's database. How many groups are represented in the database? Who has access to the database? How is the database used? How often is it updated? What are the advantages of using a database? What are the disadvantages?

2. One of the most interesting applications of computerized databases is in the sports arena. Some database programs are designed to help individual athletes, such the Sport Sight program that studies a baseball pitcher's motion or the Sports Technology program that analyzes a golfer's swing. Other programs, such as one from Sports-Tech International, are used by college and professional teams. These programs can help in evaluating players and determining how other teams handle certain situations. The Indiana Pacers credit their database programs in the selection of Kenny Williams in the draft and the defeat of Michael Jordan and the Chicago Bulls in the first six games the teams played after starting the system. Using current magazines and other resources, research the relationship between computerized databases and sports. How are databases being used? How might they be used in the future? What impact will databases have on individual and team sports?

Choosing a
Programming
Language
Summarizing the Lab
18

Instructions: Use the *Choosing a Programming Language* interactive lab to complete the following outline.

I. What is a programming language?

To communicate with a computer, a person uses a _____ — a set of written words and symbols that have meaning for the computer.

Programming is the process of writing computer programs, or the instructions that tell a computer what to do. Developing a program involves six steps: analyze the problem (define the problem and determine what needs to be done), design the program (develop a logical solution), code the program (write the instructions in a proramming language), test the program (check the instructions to make sure they work), formalize the solution (review the code and documentation), and maintain the program (identify errors and possible enhancements).

> ### Exploring Windows
> Programmers designing software for Windows must meet a detailed set of guidelines to receive approval from Microsoft, which allows them to put the Designed for Windows logo on their products. For example, programs must support long file names and be able to run under Windows NT (another Microsoft operating system) as well as Windows.

Each programming language has its own _____ , or rules, which must be followed to form meaningful program statements.

Syntax errors missed by a programmer usually are identified by the computer when it decodes the program instructions. Logic errors, which cause the wrong processing to take place, are more difficult to detect. During desk checking, programmers review the logic of a program and try to find errors, called bugs. Debugging is the process of locating and correcting program errors.

II. Types of programming languages

Programming languages fall into the categories illustrated in Figure 18.

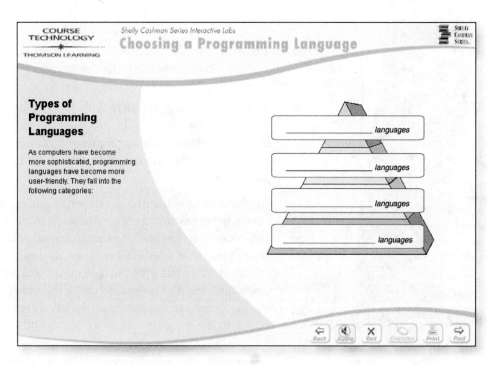

Figure 18

A. _____ is a computer's native language. It is a series of _____ representing basic operations.

Computers with different processors have different machine languages, because each microprocessor's _____ is unique.

Programs written in all other language categories are converted into machine language before they are executed.

Machine language can be very efficient because the programmer has direct control over the computer. Nevertheless, machine language programs take a long time to write, are difficult to review for errors, and can run only on specific processors.

B. _____ make machine languages easier to remember by assigning text abbreviations to each machine instruction.

An assembler is a special program that converts assembly language programs into machine language.

The abbreviations used in assembly languages are called mnemonics or symbolic operation codes. Assembly languages often include macroinstructions that generate more than one machine language instruction. Like machine languages, assembly languages are machine dependent, which means they can work only with specific hardware.

C. _____ contain nouns and verbs, similar to human languages, to make programming easier.

High-level languages are _____ , meaning that programs written using these languages can be run on many different types of computers.

The sentences in high-level language programs are called program statements. Because they are similar to human languages, high-level languages can be read by programmers and are easier to learn and use than machine or assembly languages. Although more advanced languages have been developed, high-level languages remain popular because of the large number of existing programs in which they have been used.

High-level languages are translated into machine languages in two ways: a compiler translates an entire program that is then stored for later execution; or an interpreter translates one program statement at a time, executes it, and then moves on to the next program statement. An interpreter makes it easier to find errors, but takes longer to execute an entire program than a compiler.

D. _____ , or 4GLs, are commonly described as _____ , meaning that the programmer simply communicates what tasks should be done instead of specifying the steps required to perform them.

4GLs, sometimes called very high-level languages, are described as being results oriented because programmers can specify what is to be done (usually by describing the output) without having to stipulate how it is to be done. Although they provide fewer processing options and require more computer processing power than other language generations, because of their ease of use experts predict 4GLs will continue to be popular.

A natural language, or fifth generation language, is an extension of 4GLs that allows users to enter a query as if speaking to another person.

E. _____ , or OOP, is a new trend in language design that combines data and related instructions into self-contained items called objects.

The instructions contained in an object are called _____ . New objects can re-use, or _____ , the capabilities of existing objects.

An object is part of a class, or group, with specific characteristics. An object inherits all of the methods of its class and also has methods unique to the object. As OOP is used by an organization, the organization builds up a library of OOP objects and classes. Objects can be used in different programs, which significantly reduces programming time. OOP often is described as event-driven, meaning the program responds to events that take place when an application is run and does not have to proceed from beginning to end in a linear manner.

Exploring Online

Yahoo! lists a number of sites related to programming languages such as Basic, Cobol, C, and more. JavaWorld, by contrast, is an online magazine devoted to Java. To learn more about the programming languages discussed in this chapter, visit the Exploring Computers Web page (www.scsite.com/expl.htm) and click Programming.

III. Application generators

An application generator is a _____ that enables programmers to build working programs quickly. Programmers describe the _____ , _____ , and _____ desired, and the application generator creates a suitable program. Application generators usually include tools to help programmers easily create _____ and _____ for the new program.

Application generators, also called program generators, are available as stand-alone programs or as part of other software. They use standard processing modules (such as routines to read, write, or compare records), which are stored in a library and selected and grouped together based on user specifications.

IV. Programming languages used today

Many programming languages have evolved to fulfill a variety of computing needs.

A. _____ , a high-level language designed to be easy for students to learn and use, also is used to develop business and scientific applications. Many computer systems include a customized version of BASIC.

BASIC is an easy to use, flexible language that can be used to write programs in almost any area. Most versions of BASIC are interpreted, so programmers are informed of errors instantly. BASIC has become one of the most popular programming languages and is supported by nearly every computer, although different computers may use different versions of BASIC.

B. _____ , another high-level language used for business applications, is written in sentences and paragraphs, making programs easy to read and understand. COBOL is best suited to performing _____ on large amounts of data.

COBOL is widely used, especially on large computers. As companies downsize, PC versions of COBOL have become popular. Some experts believe that COBOL has been used to write more than 75 percent of today's business software. COBOL programs can be up to seven times longer than programs written in other languages, but they are easy to debug and maintain (revise).

C. _____ , the first high-level language, is designed to be used by scientists, engineers, and mathematicians. FORTRAN is noted for its capability to express and calculate _____ easily.

Although it was developed in the 1950s, FORTRAN still is popular and can be used with almost all computers, including mainframes and personal computers. Because FORTRAN is capable of executing complex formulas, it continues to be widely employed in the scientific community.

D. The _____ language, developed as a tool for teaching programming, intentionally omits more powerful statements that may be difficult for novice programmers. Due to its highly structured syntax, Pascal encourages students to follow the principles of _____ .

Structured program design is a methodology that emphasizes professionally accepted standards and logic. These design concepts help to create programs that are easy to write, read, understand, check for errors, and maintain. Because Pascal is an excellent tool for presenting proper programming techniques, it is often a required course for computer science and information systems majors.

E. _____ , a high-level language originally developed for writing system software, has become widely used on all types of computers. Many _____ and application programs are written in C.

C offers a great deal of flexibility, and C programs are efficient and fast. C is the language preferred by many professionals who write programs for personal computers. Special effects in several films, including *Star Trek*, were developed using C.

Choosing a
Programming Language

F. _____ is a version of C enhanced with object-oriented features. Programs written in _____ can be converted to C++ and modified to take advantage of its additional features.

Like C, C++ is a powerful and efficient language but it can be difficult to learn. Object-oriented programming requires a differ- ent approach from procedural programming, and traditional programmers sometimes have trouble using the object-oriented char-acteristics of C++. Despite this, C++ is used frequently to develop application software.

G. _____ enable programmers to create graphical, object-oriented programs for the Windows environment. These languages feature object-oriented tools and help programmers build _____ into their programs.

H. _____ is a simple object-oriented programming language developed by Sun Microsystems that can be used to develop programs able to be delivered over the Internet. An _____ is a Java program that can be included in a Web page and viewed using a Web browser.

I. _____ is a special formatting language used to cre-ate Web pages. HTML uses _____ to specify links as well as how a Web page displays.

Dynamic HTML (DTML) is a newer type of HTML that allows you to include more interest and interactivity on a Web page, without the Web page accessing the Web server.

Exploring Your Computer

Your computer runs a variety of programs written in a various programming languages. For example, both Microsoft and Lotus have developed application software using C. *Exploring Computers*, the program that is currently running on your computer, was developed using Macromedia Director, a multimedia authoring program written in C++.

V. Choosing a language

Choosing a language for the solution to a programming task depends on many factors: _____ , _____ , _____ , and _____ .

A. The organization that will use the new program may have a _____ specifying the language used for all programs.

B. A new program must be able to _____ efficiently with existing programs, which may be easier if all programs are written in the same language.

C. Different programming languages are better _____ to solving some problems than others.

D. _____ means that a program can run on different computer platforms without modification.

A final consideration is the expertise of available programmers. Unless another language is far superior, it is best to choose a language with which programmers are comfortable.

Evaluating the Results

True/False

Instructions: Circle **T** if the statement is true or **F** if the statement is false.

T F 1. As computers have become more sophisticated, programming languages have become less user-friendly.

T F 2. Computers with different processors have the same machine language because all processors have identical instruction sets.

T F 3. High-level languages commonly are described as machine-dependent, meaning that a program written in a high-level language can be run on only one type of computer.

T F 4. In the traditional programming model, data and the instructions that operate on the data are kept separate.

T F 5. With OOP, new types of data can re-use, or inherit, the capabilities of existing data types.

Matching

Instructions: Write the letter of a description from the column on the right in front of each term in the left column on the left.

_____ 1. BASIC

_____ 2. COBOL

_____ 3. Java

_____ 4. Pascal

_____ 5. C

a. an object-oriented language, used to write programs for delivery over the Internet

b. a fourth-generation language used with artificial intelligence applications

c. a high-level language best suited to performing simple calculations on large amounts of data

d. a high-level language originally designed for writing system software

e. a high-level language designed to simplify the preparation of business reports

f. a high-level language designed to be easy for students to learn and use

g. a highly-structured language developed as a tool for teaching programming

Multiple Choice

Instructions: Circle the correct response.

1. Into what language must all programs be translated before they run?
    a. machine language
    b. assembly language
    c. high-level language
    d. fourth-generation language

2. How is object-oriented programming different from traditional programming?
    a. instructions are arranged in sentences and grouped into paragraphs
    b. programmers must specify the procedures used to accomplish a task
    c. data and related instructions are combined into self-contained items
    d. abbreviations are used to represent machine operation code

3. What language intentionally omits program statements that may be difficult for novice programmers and encourages students to follow the principles of structured program design?
    a. FORTRAN
    b. Pascal
    c. COBOL
    d. C

4. What are visual languages?
    a. languages that display all necessary characters and symbols on the computer screen
    b. languages that use lines between program statements to illustrate relationships
    c. languages that help programmers build graphical user interfaces into their programs
    d. languages that show the result of a program statement immediately after it is entered

5. Which of the following is not a factor in choosing a programming language?
    a. the necessity for the application to be portable
    b. the programming standards of the organization
    c. the need to isolate new programs from existing programs
    d. the suitability to the application being programmed

Fill in the Blanks

Instructions: Place the correct word(s) in the blank in each sentence.

1. A(n) _____ is a set of written words and symbols that have meaning for the computer.

2. Each programming language has its own _____ , or rules, which must be followed to form meaningful program statements.

3. Assembly language programs are converted into machine language by a special program called a(n) _____ .

4. Fourth-generation languages commonly are described as _____ , which means programmers simply communicate what should be done instead of specifying the steps required.

5. A(n) _____ is a program builder that produces programs in other languages.

Examining the Issues

1. When computers were first introduced in schools, computer programming was routinely taught to students at all levels. As time passed, however, the emphasis in computer instruction turned toward application software. People felt programs had already been written for just about every imaginable task, and it was more important to teach students how to use the tools available. Today, however, that trend is changing. More educators are teaching programming languages such as Cobol, Visual Basic, C++, and Java. They believe that programming should still be an integral part of computer education. How might knowledge of programming benefit computer users? Should programming in some form be a part of computer education? Why or why not? To whom should programming be taught?

2. Because each programming language has its own strengths and weaknesses, different languages are used for different applications. Some authorities believe, however, it would be best to develop a single programming language that could be used for all applications. What would be the advantage of writing all applications using the same programming language? What would be the disadvantages? Will a generic programming language ever be developed? Why or why not?

Investigating World
the

1. Some applications come with programming languages (sometimes called macro languages) that can be used to write programs within the application. For example, Microsoft Excel, a spreadsheet program, and Microsoft Word, a word processing program, both include Visual Basic for Applications (VBA). Visit a software vendor and find an application that contains a programming language. What is the name of the application? What is the name of the programming language? For what purpose is the language used? If possible, ask to see a demonstration of the programming language. Does it appear difficult to use? Why or why not? Would the inclusion of a programming language in an application be a factor in your decision whether or not to purchase the software? Why?

2. Careers in programming are hotter than ever: estimates anticipate that from the year 1992 to the year 2005 there will be a 30 percent increase in the number of programmer positions available. What knowledge and skills are required to land one of these jobs? Using classified ads from newspapers, computer magazines, trade journals, or other resources, try to determine what employers are looking for in prospective programmers. What programming languages are most in demand? What other skills and course work are required? What kind of experience is helpful? What are the programmer's responsibilities? What salary can be expected? What are the opportunities for advancement?

Index

Dialog box, 1.5, 1.6
DIMM packages, 7.5
Direct-access storage devices, 11.2
Disabled users, voice input and, 14.2
Disk management, operating system, 12.5
Display, configuring, 10.1-8. *See also* Monitors
Display adapters, 15.3
Documents
 printing, 9.1-10
 scanning, 8.1-8
 turnaround, 8.2
 word processing, 5.1-2
Domain, 3.2
Dot matrix printers, 9.1
Dots per inch (dpi), 8.5, 9.2, 10.4
Double-click, 1.4
Downloaded font, 9.6
Draft quality printing, 9.1
Drag-and-drop editing, 5.3, 9.6
Dragging, 1.4, 1.5
Drivers
 operating system and, 12.4
 printer, 9.4
Drop-down list, 1.6
Dynamic HTML (DHTML), 18.6

Ecological issues, printers and, 9.10
Editing
 drag-and-drop, 5.3, 9.6
 online, 5.4
 word processing and, 5.3
Education
 computer requirements, 14.11
 computer-assisted instruction, 14.6, 14.12
 multimedia and, 15.5
 programming, 18.11
 Web-based, 14.6
Edutainment, 15.6
Electronic mail, *see* E-mail
Electronic spreadsheet, 6.1
E-mail, 3.1-2, 14.4
 viruses and, 16.3
E-mail etiquette, 3.2
Emotional problems, computers and, 13.9
ENIAC, 7.9
ENTER key, 2.5
 spreadsheet and, 6.4
Entertainment
 multimedia and, 15.5, 15.6
 software, 14.6
Ergonomics, 13.1-10
Europe, word processing software and, 5.9
Excel, 6.5, 6.10, 18.12
Executable files, viruses in, 16.2
Expansion bus, 7.6
Expansion slots, 7.6
Eyes, protecting, 13.4

Favorites, 4.4
Fiber-optic cable, 14.3
Fifth generation language, 18.3
File management, operating system and, 12.5
File Transfer Protocol, *see* FTP
Files
 audio, 15.2
 compressed, 3.2, 11.4, 15.3-4
 database, 17.1-2, 17.5
 deleted, 11.8
 flat, 17.2, 17.6, 17.9
 FTP, 3.2
 graphics, 8.2
 hard disk storage, 11.4
 spreadsheet, 6.1-2
 video, 15.3
 viruses and, 16.2, 16.4
 Web pages, 4.1
Find feature, 5.3
Flat files, 17.2, 17.6, 17.9
Floppy disk, 11.2, 11.5
 viruses and, 16.4
Floppy disk drives, 7.2, 11.1, 11.4
Fonts, 5.4-5
 printing and, 9.3, 9.5-6
Footer, 5.6
Formatting
 spreadsheets and, 6.4
 templates and, 5.9
 word processing document, 5.4-5, 5.6
Formatting disks, 11.3
Formulas, 6.3, 6.4
 built-in, 6.5
FORTRAN, 18.5
Fourth generation language (4GL), 18.3
Fragmentation, of hard disk, 11.4-5
FTP (File Transfer Protocol), 3.2
Function keys, 2.2, 2.4
Functions, 6.5
Future, computers and, 14.1-12

Garbage In, Garbage Out (GIGO), 8.8
Gas plasma screens, 10.2
Gateway, 3.6
Goal seeking, 6.5
Grammar checker, 5.4
Graphical user interface (GUI), 1.3, 1.10, 12.3, 12.6
Graphics
 display and, 10.3-4
 files, 8.2
 multimedia and, 15.1, 15.3
 word processing programs and, 5.5
Graphics card, 7.4, 10.4-5
Graphs, spreadsheet, 6.6
Grayscale images
 printing, 9.6
 scanning, 8.4

Proportional spacing, 5.5
Protection, cell, 6.4

Quattro Pro, 6.5, 6.10
Query, database, 17.4-5

RAM, 7.2, 7.9
  speed, 7.5
  Windows and, 7.4
Range, 6.3
Read/write heads, 11.2, 11.3
Records, 17.1
Recycling paper, 9.9
Registry, 12.2
Relational database, 17.3
Relative reference, 6.4
Repetitive stress injury, 13.3, 13.5, 13.9
Replace feature, 5.3
Rescue disk, 16.4
Resolution
  graphics cards and, 10.5
  monitor, 10.4
  printers, 9.2, 10.4
  scanning and, 8.5
RGB monitors, 10.3
Right-drag, 1.5
Risk analysis, 6.9
Robots, 14.7
ROM, 7.4-5, 7.9
ROM chips, 12.2
Router, 3.5
Rows, spreadsheet, 6.2

Saving word processing document, 5.6
Scanners, 1.3, 8.1-8
Screen, 10.1-2
Scroll arrows, 5.2, 6.2
Scroll bars, 5.2, 6.2
Scroll boxes, 6.2
SCSI (small computer standard interface), 8.4
Search tools, 3.3, 4.5, 4.9
Searching
  database, 17.4-5
  Internet, 3.3, 4.5, 4.9
  word processor and, 5.3-4
Sector, 11.4
Security, data, 11.8, 12.4, 12.5, 17.1, 17.2, 17.5, 17.9
Seek time, 11.2
Sequential access storage devices, 11.4
Serial Line Internet Protocol (SLIP), 3.5
Serial ports, 7.3
Server, Internet, 3.5
Settings command (Start menu), mouse properties, 1.5
Shadow mask, 10.3
Shell program, 12.5
SHIFT key, 2.3
Shortcut menus, 5.3
SIMM packages, 7.5
Single-tasking operating systems, 12.5

Sitting, at computer, 13.2-3
SLIP (Serial Line Internet Protocol), 3.5
Smart cards, 14.1
Smart home, 14.5
Socket, 7.2
Sorting database, 17.6
Sound card, 15.2
Source data collection, 8.1
Speakers, multimedia and, 15.5
Spell checker, 5.4
Spiders, 4.9
Sports databases, 17.10
Spreadsheets, 6.1-10
  changing data in, 6.5
  effective, 6.9
Start menu, Settings command, mouse properties
  and, 1.5
Startup disk, 16.4
Storage
  capacity, 11.4
  hard drive, 11.1-8
Structured program design, 18.5
Style
  of text, 9.5-6
  word processing document and, 5.6
Surfing, 4.2
SVGA (Super Video Graphics Array), 10.5
Symmetric multiprocessing, 12.7
Syntax errors, 18.2
System bus, 7.5
System clock, 7.4
System configuration information, 12.2
System resource management, 12.3
System software, 12.1
System unit, 7.1

TAB key, 2.5
Tabs, spreadsheet, 6.2
Tags, 4.2
Telecommuting, 14.5
Telephone lines, connecting to Internet using, 3.4-5
Telephone network, fiber-optic cable and, 14.3
Templates
  voice, 14.2
  word processing, 5.6, 5.9
Text
  in cells, 6.3
  multimedia and, 15.1
  printing, 9.5
Text links, 15.2
Thermal printer, 9.3
Time bombs, 16.2
Time slice, 12.4
Timesharing, 12.6
Trackballs, 1.4, 1.10
Tracks, 11.3, 11.4
Tracks per inch (tpi), 11.4
Training, multimedia used for, 15.5, 15.9
Turnaround documents, 8.2